CONFIDENT WIZARD

HOW TO LEAD WITH AUTHENTICITY, PURPOSE, AND RESILIENCE

MARLENE GONZALEZ

LIFE COACHING GROUP LLC

CONTENTS

This book is dedicated to every person of any race or age who dreams of unlocking the leader in them. The next generation of leaders: on your shoulders lays the responsibility to build a better world.

This book is dedicated to my husband, Carlos, you are my rock and thought partner. Thanks for your love and support. My sister, Vanessa, for her unconditional support in making my dream to write this series of coaching eBooks possible.

This book is also dedicated to the Hispanic Alliance for Career Enhancement (HACE), a national non-profit dedicated to the employment, development, and advancement of Latino professionals. To all alumni, mentors, clients, and friends and family. My nieces and nephews (I would like to give you an additional edge as some of you are starting your professional journey). To my publishing team (Nick, Myra, Kevin, Susan, Fahi and Dwinny and AIA Team and Publishing Life Services), you are awesome.

JOIN OUR COMMUNITY

Please, don't make the journey alone.

In order to maximize your investment in this book, I encourage you to join our support community on our website www.marlenegonzalez.com.

It is a support group where to share and learn leadership experience and valuable content. We often host free book/audiobook giveaways and helpful resources that will be key to your leadership journey.

It will be great to connect with you there,

Your coach, Marlene Gonzalez

"It is in the leader's inner world that the game is either won or lost. There, he becomes mediocre or transcends the ordinary; his choice."

— ANONYMOUS

INTRODUCTION

In biology, metamorphosis is the striking change of form or structure in an individual after birth or hatching. Butterflies become butterflies through metamorphosis, but let's start at the beginning. All butterflies begin as an egg. The female butterfly picks a good-looking plant for her offspring and lays eggs there. A caterpillar eats its way out of the egg in a few days to begin its new journey. It spends most of its time eating — caterpillars eat leaves of all kinds. The caterpillar's appetite allows it to get everything it needs to grow. When they are not eating, they are hiding from a predator or resting. When the caterpillar is full, it finds a nice spot to transform. It sheds its skin again, and the new skin formed is called a chrysalis.

In the final stage of metamorphosis, the caterpillar grows inside the hard shell — the chrysalis. The caterpillar grows an abdomen, legs, and wings. As it grows, the chrysalis does not expand. The caterpillar grows until it finally breaks out of the shell. The transformation takes up to two weeks, after which it emerges from the chrysalis as a butterfly.

When the chrysalis first breaks open, it hangs on the caterpillar like a small sack until its transformation into a butterfly is complete. The casual observer may see this and think that because it is motionless, nothing is happening. However, a lot is going on beneath the surface. Inside the chrysalis, the structure of the caterpillar is broken down and rearranged into what we see as a butterfly. The process of metamorphosis has a lot happening behind the scenes to transform the caterpillar into a beautiful butterfly.

But what in the world has metamorphosis to do with leadership?

Imagine the caterpillar crawling about her business, content to roam the earth on her belly, until one day she feels the call — the call to start building, the call to transform. Does she know what she is building? Does she know her destiny, or does she simply listen to the whispers of her heart and follow them until she gets tightly wrapped in her chrysalis? As she lets herself be wrapped and molded, does she realize that she is sprouting wings to fly?

In many ways, the questions you would ask of a caterpillar becoming a butterfly are the same questions you would ask of someone growing into a leader. Like the caterpillar, they must heed the call to transform themselves from the ordinary to embrace the leader within. You have to heed the divine call and courageously step up, saying, "I am prepared to become who I was meant to be."

Transformation is not about popularity, wealth, or fame. It is about becoming more and more authentic, whole, loving, and complete. It is about living a meaningful life and fulfilling your life's purpose. It is about listening to the whispers and attending to what you know to be right. It is about transforming into who you really are so that you can appreciate the bad together with the good and embrace opportunities to grow.

Many people talk about leadership, but few of them talk about the inner game of leading. Yet, success comes from within. It is in the leader's inner world that the game is either won or lost. Too often, people focus on the visible manifestation of leadership — actions, gestures, habits, and styles — and these matter but the real work of leadership is forged in our minds. It is unseen by all except the individual who is fighting with self-doubt and all other internal battles.

Every person who has held a leadership role or a position of influence knows this to be true. They are familiar with the battle that rages in their minds as they try to deal with the uncertainties and ambiguity of life. They know that to be effective as leaders, they must win in that space between their ears where no one sees. They know that the narrative that plays in their minds is of paramount importance if they are to succeed. At the very heart of this inner game is self-confidence.

Self-confidence is the spring from which bubbles all the visible aspects of leadership. It feeds effectiveness, people management, competence, skill development, and conflict resolution, to name a few. This is why self-confidence is vital to the meaning of true leadership.

Think back to when someone told you that you were smart, charismatic, kind, or inspiring. How did you respond? How do you take compliments? When people praise us or recognize our capabilities and skills, it can boost our confidence — *as long as we believe those good things too.* Doubting the good things people say about you is the opposite of self-confidence. To feel truly confident, you need to believe you are capable.

But what is confidence? Where does it come from? How is it developed? As a leader, ask yourself, "What can I do to help build my self-confidence because it affects me and others around me?" A confident person feels and shows confidence in themselves. They are self-assured. Let me share a story to illustrate:

Caroline is the general manager in a logistics and procurement company. When she was promoted, her direct reports increased over 10 times, expanding the range of business processes she oversaw. Naturally, she felt a bit shaky about the move. Caroline is strongly convicted about collaborative and transparent leadership, so she opened her heart to her new employees:

"I want to do this job, but I am a little scared, and I need you to help me."

Her honesty backfired, causing her to lose credibility with her team who wanted a confident leader to step in and take the reins.

Or take Jack, a Nigerian executive in an auto parts business where people like to have a clear chain of command and make their decisions democratically. When a United States-based company with a matrix structure bought the company, he found himself working with colleagues who handled decision-making like a casual contest for controversial ideas. Having to debate did not come easily to Jack. It went against all he knew about humility — learned from his home country. In a company-wide debrief, his boss let him know that he needed to be more vocal about his accomplishments and ideas. Jack felt like he had to pick between being a fake and a failure.

What do these two stories tell you about confidence?

For starters, confidence cannot be divorced from authenticity. Thanks to a change in how people view leadership, technological advances, and social media attention, authenticity is becoming the gold standard for leadership.

Recently, the term "authenticity," has faced a public relations crisis. It seems to have lost meaning because it is ubiquitous on business and personal blogs and style magazines. It can appear as if everyone wants this virtue, yet many people preaching its virtue do not understand the word well. What does authenticity really mean? How do you practice it in leadership?

Undoubtedly, a simplistic understanding of what authenticity is can get in the way of growth and stymie your impact. Like with Jack, going against our natural tendencies can make us feel like impostors, and so we often use authenticity as an excuse not to leave our comfort zone. Yet, few jobs allow you to be comfortable for long. That is even true as you move up your career or when the expectations of the job change, and your confidence is put to the test.

As a leader who is newly promoted, it is not easy to inspire your team. There is always an anxiety that comes with the increased responsibility and questions you have to answer. How do you bring ideas up with credibility? How do you make the difficult choices? What about your team? How do you rally them if they were formerly your peers or if they do not know you at all? After gaining your promotion, your responsibilities and exposure increase. You have high expectations, but you realize that there is much you do not know. How do you avoid making the same mistake Caroline made?

Perhaps, you want to increase the productivity of your startup. Maybe you are an entrepreneur who wants to understand the true meaning of self-leadership and leading from within. Maybe you only want to improve yourself to reach your future goals. You want to grow into all that you can be and have the most impact you know yourself to be capable of having in the world. You want to become a butterfly.

In this book, you will discover how to transform your leadership skills so that you can motivate, inspire and encourage. It takes a true leader to guide a team to success. You cannot be successful in your leadership if you constantly struggle with low self-esteem and low self-awareness. How do you express your inner convictions and live out your values and purpose if you have no confidence? How do you embody thoughtful leadership, stress resilience, and authenticity?

You will learn what authenticity is and how to achieve it with confidence and conviction. If you are looking for purpose, inspiration, and meaning in your life, this book is for you. Do you wish to gain an edge in your leadership performance? Are you overwhelmed by burnout or stress? What do you do when that happens? How do you increase self-awareness and your inner resources to achieve the things that matter most to you? How do you become more confident?

Confidence does not just happen. You become more confident when you commit to being more confident and set the intention. Then, you have to put attention into developing and sustaining the right behavior over time. It will be trying, and it will push you beyond your comfort zone, but it will also be rewarding. Nothing is out of reach for a confident person. This book will help you figure out how to go about building your confidence. You will learn about the importance of being an inspiring leader and how to build your authentic self and lead with a clear overall purpose for your life.

As an author and executive coach, I know that you must first be open-minded to become more authentic — and expect the same from others. You attract the things you want in life when you are receptive. I have had to apply this principle to my experience in the business world, from exploring new ways to work with employees to collaborating with organizations that may never otherwise have been on my radar. I am the president and founder of LCG Group LLC. I spend my days coaching and helping people develop their leadership skills. I have partnered with many organizations and teams to help them meet common leadership challenges and harness them to achieve success.

Few things give me as much joy as watching talented professionals develop their skills and identify their values. I have been studying and researching issues for years to understand what makes true leaders and have used my lessons in my practice. Helping you to get the skills you need to become a confident leader matters deeply to me, which is why I have packed this book with information to help you to encourage, inspire and guide you to find your authentic self and lead with purpose and resilience.

Throughout my practice, I have had people approach me and ask me how I got to be so confident, especially when coaching, speaking in public, or taking up leadership roles. The reality is that I used to struggle with self-confidence. I doubted myself, my skills, talents, and accomplishments and had a persistent negative voice feeding my fears and making me feel like a fraud. I had to work very hard to become a confident wizard, get out of my comfort zone, and try new things. It was difficult to stand up for myself and express my true feelings because I feared what others would think.

I understand that it is a natural thing to desire authenticity. We want to know that the people we bring into our space embody that as well. Here, you will learn how to become truly yourself, and, as a result, become the best leader you could be as you lead from within. You will discover eight key dimensions to successfully unlock your authentic power by looking within yourself.

Learning what it means to succeed as a transformational leader is an art form that you can master and use to infuse your team with dignity and pride. It doesn't matter where you are in your career. Finding your inspiration, building your character, and following the strategies in this book will bring you closer to your goals. All you need is drive, confidence, and mindfulness to get to the same level as the successful leaders you admire.

You will realize that being a confident leader is not about having all the answers. The opposite is true. Confident leaders leverage the knowledge and expertise of their team. They are not fearful of asking for help and admitting mistakes because they learned from them. They are confident in making decisions and are decisive when making the right choice even when it's unpopular.

Confident leaders are not about accolades. They are humble, yet self-assured. A type of leader who is charismatic develops and supports their team. They are not afraid of letting others grow and are comfortable that their employees may be better than themselves. Knowing what you stand for will ensure that you make decisions based on your values, not your circumstances. Otherwise, your choices will be reactionary and inconsistent.

Here, beginning today, you can become the leader you were meant to be. You can tap into leadership skills hidden within you and rally your team behind you toward success. Packed with stories, practices, and tools to help you lead from within, this book is your guide to becoming a transformational leader and unlocking your potential. It will help you to look inward and tap into the wisdom found within in a journey of self-discovery and self-awareness, growing in authenticity and learning to always stay true to your values. You will develop a clear purpose and learn how to continually renew it so that your fears and limiting beliefs will never hold you back again.

Undergoing this process requires faith. It requires listening to the whispers of your heart and heeding to the desire to transform. It is a journey to find the divine within and become the butterfly you are destined to be. In this book, you will learn how to build and enter your chrysalis. You will understand the time and work that is required to grow your wings. You will understand the process of change and the need for practice. Then, you will begin to believe in yourself so that you do not overstay your welcome in the chrysalis. Finally, you emerge as a butterfly. This is a book that will help you fly.

1

THE TRUE MEANING OF A LEADER

Have you ever wondered what makes a true leader?

Pick a person at random and ask them to tell you some leaders they admire. They will likely mention some obvious and well-known people, but eventually, they get around to less famous people who they know in person and have worked with. For some people, it is a parent or a relative who they lived with. For others, it is a colleague or a leader in their workplace, but it is always someone they interact with regularly.

Suppose you probe further and ask what they admire about these leaders. In that case, you will likely hear words like vision, persona, confidence, perseverance, a winning attitude, and coping with adversity. What is interesting is that all the responses will describe behavior. This should not be surprising. Whether you are a great leader or not, you can see that people respond to how you behave, not your wits.

You must wonder, "How do you get there?". Being a confident leader is more complex than anyone has ever imagined. Many concepts about leadership miss the mark because they assume that to be a great leader, you must be like person X, who did extraordinary things. True, one aspect of leadership is learning from others, which may demand that you imitate their choices at some point, but more crucial is the ability to be who you truly are. It is the ability to influence others from the core of who they are. True leaders know how to stay true to their values and still get things done. They know that they do not have to sacrifice themselves to achieve the extraordinary.

You will succeed as a leader if you learn how to be true to who you are, inspire others and create a safe space for them to grow and prosper. True leaders lead from within. They have a high level of self-awareness, conviction, clarity and are always on purpose.

Here is a short story to illustrate this:

The person who learns to tap into their internal resources, who can lean into their strengths and work to improve their weaknesses, will almost inevitably prevail against every situation life throws at them. You can be a confident leader without competing against someone else. A leader who inspires the people around them and helps them "deal with" challenging times has first learned to "get through" challenging times. They have learned how to make themselves well-rounded and focused and how to infuse that into their team.

Authenticity is a trait that all self-aware leaders need to have and embody in their leadership styles. When you are authentic, your speech is true to who you are, and you can genuinely care for your employees and your team. You know what to say and how to say it. When you speak up, you mean it. You not only inspire your team but also have a structure in place that tracks success. What does it mean to inspire, though?

Inspiration depends on the leader, but it comes from understanding your person and your purpose. You have a true north that you align with every day. It is about knowing what it is that makes you unique as a leader. True leaders follow a clear path to understand their beliefs, attitudes, values, courage, authenticity, and sense of hope. This book is your guide to help you do just that. It is not meant to do the work for you but to help you do the work efficiently.

The good thing is that you are working on yourself when the world is friendly to people who find out the uniqueness they bring and embrace it. Generation Z kids have never lived without social media; smartphones and the internet have many opportunities and advantages. They are highly motivated to make changes in the world and are interested in social issues. Research has found that few other generations are as socially conscious as Generation Z.

GENERATION Z KIDS WHO HAVE MADE A DIFFERENCE IN THE WORLD

Jesse Kay is a 21-year-old entrepreneur from New Jersey. He is also a public speaker and a podcaster. Jesse started doing business from an early age, launching his first business in 2009 when he was just 9. At the time, his business included flipping shoes on eBay. When Jesse was in junior high, he began his podcast, *20 under the 20s*, where he interviewed successful people. He sent 350 emails every day while launching the podcast to reach the guests he wanted. Over time, he interviewed Paul Rodriguez, Gary Vaynerchuk, and Jack Dorsey, among others, for more than 100 000 listeners.

For Jesse, the podcast is about sharing practical stories and lessons from the world's best minds to help inspire young women and men to become the entrepreneurs of tomorrow. He has been featured in many global publications, including *Adweek, HuffPost, Entrepreneur,* and *Business Insider.* In addition to his podcast, he has spoken across North America and is part of a digital consulting agency helping Fortune 500 brands, including the New York Rangers and New York Knicks, connect with their young customers and fans through digital marketing and social media.

Stories like Jesse's happen only for those who recognize what they bring to the world and are unafraid to step out and provide it. What did Jesse have that you do not? He believed in and worked from his beliefs, attitudes, and values to make his vision a reality. He embodied the necessary courage to be authentic, and with a sense of hope, he made a difference. In this book, you will learn how you can become a self-aware leader. You will find several lessons on how to grow the confidence to lead.

Being self-aware is one of the most significant steps you can take to become a leader. To properly travel the path of self-discovery to become a truly transformational leader, you must discover the underlying issues you need to tackle. Sometimes, the things standing between you and what you want are hiding under the surface. They look like habits or decisions that you do not have to work very hard to make. They simply click in when the situation calls for it, but they keep you in an unproductive loop.

If people were born with an instructional manual, it would teach them how to lead themselves. It would contain pointers and directions on how to persevere when faced with challenges, and it would teach you how to handle your emotions. The instruction manual would certainly equip you on how to pick a goal — the right goal for you — and how to do everything necessary to meet it, all the while helping those around you with theirs. As it is though, no one is born with one. You must learn from others, and sometimes through mistakes, to govern yourself and lead yourself into the place you were meant to be. You must begin by becoming self-aware.

Self-awareness is an aspect of self-leadership. It is the process of knowing who you are, finding your desired experiences, and intentionally moving toward them. It is about applying your signature strengths to begin, maintain and sustain self-influencing behaviors. Basic self-awareness is necessary to understand your needs, drives, and motives. With self-awareness, you know your personality traits, which explain your feelings, thoughts, and behavior. You understand why you have certain tendencies and why some things come easy to you. You will be able to identify when your actions are aligned with your core values and when you are self-sabotaging.

It is also about knowing your strengths and weaknesses, values, interests, and talents. That way, you know what you find interesting and can identify and manage things you find draining. Self-awareness helps you make decisions based on the things that are most important to you and know how to use your talents to maximize your chances of success. People with self-knowledge can tell what they are feeling and why, what is important to them, and their sense of purpose.

THE CORE COMPETENCIES AND SKILLS OF A TRUE LEADER

In the book *Man's Search for Meaning,* Viktor E. Frankl survived the Holocaust and years of incarceration in a Nazi concentration camp. Despite hardships, he thrived. Frankl demonstrated many skills all through his experience. He understood what he could change and what he could not. He realized that only he could decide how to respond to things happening around him. Frankl may not have had much control over external factors, but he could use his internal resources to make a difference.

Frankl understood the importance of having values in life. He had a sustaining awareness of his values and chose to live by them, giving him a sense of purpose and meaning. He demonstrated constructive thought strategies and continually saw opportunities to make his fellow inmates better. Because of this, he managed to persevere throughout his incarceration and afterward. This is the essence of a true leader. A true leader leads themselves. They display the following core skills and competencies:

They know their desired experiences.

By nature, people strive for happiness, and goals are the channel for it. Without goals, no one can be happy. Yet, research shows that a person's ability to know what would make them happy is not developed (Covey, 2009). The true leader understands how to align their goals with their values. That way, they are motivated to pursue their goals. They recognize opportunities to live in line with what they believe across different areas in life.

They are constructive in their thoughts and decision-making.

Have you ever noticed how you respond to stress? Research shows that most people cannot think critically when they are under stress. (Festinger, 1957). We are neurologically wired to perceive a threat. We have to be proactive to become positive in our thinking. The true leader knows this. They have a growth mindset and are always choosing how to react to their experiences. They cultivate positivity and mindfulness.

They plan and set goals.

Goal setting and planning is about atomizing your bigger dreams into manageable milestones, then making the best of each one. True leaders plan and commit to proactively document their work, setting up accountability and the positive reward they will attach to reaching their goal.

They optimize motivation.

The true leader adjusts their goals to make them more appealing. They take advantage of their intrinsically motivating goals, values, and self-concept to power through their milestones. They understand the role that willpower plays in achieving success. They try new behaviors and understand the value of taking small, yet continuous steps.

They harness the ecosystem.

The true leader harnesses their nature. Having done the work to understand who they are, they can rely on their strengths to propel them forward. They proactively seek support for their goal behavior in their physical, political, organizational, and social environment. This could mean anything from mobilizing social support to changing their physical environment to support a goal they are pursuing, like removing junk food from the fridge when trying to eat healthily.

They amplify their performance.

The true leader knows the conditions they need to perform at optimum. They seek solutions where they are stuck, and they take advantage of tools that make them perform better. They accept it when they fail and look instead to cultivate grit. True leaders stick to their plans. They know what adjustments to make to their expectations when they encounter failure. They are adept at self-compassion.

As you read this book, assess what it may take you to become a more confident leader and how you can manifest those qualities and improve your skills to inspire your teams to do great things. You will go down a path to determine your own identity and your underlying purpose to break into the inspirational and transformational role of a leader. Explore how a leader's personal beliefs and values can help shape a team of competent experts. This can be one of the determining factors of your mission and vision for the future, and you will understand the true meaning of authenticity and courage that will help you become the leader you've always wanted to be.

True leaders are only true when they are genuinely themselves. In walking this journey of self-discovery, you will be setting yourself up for success. One day, you will tell the story of how you grew into yourself, and it will be another person's survival guide. But first, you have to tap into your inner strength. You have to face yourself and embrace your story. This will be discussed in-depth in the next chapter.

TRUE LEADERSHIP ACTIVITIES

A true leader knows how to set goals that are aligned with their vision. They know that there is more involved in leadership than power, a title, and managing others. He constantly works to develop his capacity to lead. The following activities will help you further reflect on what you think about leadership and your ideal leadership style.

1. Find Leaders You Admire

Without overthinking, list two to five leaders you admire on a piece of paper. What do you like about them? What makes them great leaders? Highlight common traits between them and any desirable characteristics they possess. What could you emulate from them?

2. Describe the Idea: You as a Leader

Suppose you had all your ducks lined in a row; you are finally in your dream job and are managing the team you have always wanted. What would that look like? If you were not occasionally nervous, unsure, confused, and tired, how would you lead? Describe it in as much detail as you can.

3. Question Journaling

Journal about these three questions: (You will expand on the answers to these questions as you continue with this exercise.)

- *Who am I?*
- *How can I better know myself?*
- *What do I stand for?*

Please note, all activities in this book, or workbook if you prefer, are tied together. They aim at making you the person you were meant to be. It is a worthy investment to take some time on each.

2

YOUR PERSONAL STORY

What exactly do you want from your life? If you could have the life you wanted, how would it look? What kind of person would you be? How would you respond to conflict? What things would you pursue relentlessly, and what would you choose to leave to others? Answering these questions is the essence of having personal values. In answering them, you will know where you are going and why. You will be able to tell when a decision is right for you and when it is not. Having personal values will help you understand what authenticity looks like for you.

Personal values, dreams, talents, and even your personality traits may not always seem like they count in the rush of daily life. It is easy to begin getting through what needs doing without much thought, but an awareness of these things can give insight into your inner self. Daily priorities are undoubtedly important, but life becomes about going through the motions without much enjoyment if you do not have a sense of meaning. This chapter will provide you with the tools you need in your self-discovery journey. It will help you to know who you are a little better.

Self-discovery is about examining your life, figuring out what is lacking, and taking the necessary steps toward fulfillment, and there is no better time to explore yourself than the present. In taking the journey, you set yourself up to become a leader who leads from within. You make sure that your choices are good on a number of levels. They are good for you in the present in that they have your interests at heart. They are good for the future you and who you want to become, and they are also good for the people around you both in the present and in the future.

Confident wizards should follow a motto that helps them lead with the authenticity, purpose, and resilience they have always desired. They are driven from within, but what exactly does that mean? When you are leading from within, you broadcast and project the things that you genuinely believe. You make decisions based on your core values. As such, anything could define a person as a leader because they believe in it and transmit that passion.

As you lead from within, you must not only project your beliefs but also pass your talents and have your team know exactly why you are driven to achieve your goals. It is about shaping a group that will take on your legacy and carry your leadership styles to the next team. The effects of leading from within ripple down through generations, so self-discovery is an important starting point. It is an integral component of personal growth. It is a way you explore your personalities, values, natural preferences, beliefs, and tendencies. Here is a short story to illustrate this:

Catherine was 14 when she tried to starve herself thin. By age 23, she was adept at covering up her body image issues by lying to herself. As Catherine went on a journey of self-discovery, she realized that pretending the feeling did not exist was not helping her. It had become exhausting. She could no longer act as if she was just okay. Social interactions were getting harder and so were other regular things like dressing up.

Catherine accepted that she had body image issues, which was the first step toward a better life. Soon, she was no longer living in fear. Being true to her feelings, acknowledging them, and validating them had set her free. Rather than constantly fret that she was not living up to her expectations, she began jogging every morning. The fear that was holding her back became the fuel for her morning runs. After she became conscious of her real beliefs, they no longer strangled her. She could finally change what she did not like. Catherine committed to getting fit and she is an inspiration for her team and others.

As a person, the more you know who you are and what you stand for, the less likely you are to do things because other people are doing them. You become more secure in yourself. As a leader, rather than passively going through life and reacting to whatever challenges you encounter, you actively look to make a difference.

It is easy to keep checking the boxes that define success by everyone else's standards. It is also easy to climb the corporate ladder and then realize that you have been wandering aimlessly. What do you do when you realize how misaligned you are? How do you begin to collect the pieces of who you once were and re-order them to someone you can learn to respect again? How do you walk back to where you began to miss the mark and make the necessary changes? The answer lies in self-discovery.

Earlier, we described self-discovery as the process of self-reflection that allows you to figure out what you believe and who you are. The part the definition left out is that self-discovery is an ongoing process. You could begin your leadership journey utterly aware of who you are and what you stand for but then lose your way along the process. What then? The system in this book and the recommendations work every time. They will always lead you toward your true purpose and enable you to express who you are and who you want to be in the future.

It is self-discovery that shows you where to go from where you are. It stops you from just living for others, which will never create the impact you want. In one study about knowing yourself done by Cambridge University, Jordan Mackenzie argues that we are in an unavoidable relationship with ourselves that demands self-respect and self-love (2018). Self-love gives us a reason to know who we are, while self-respect demands that we take the reason seriously. Therefore, to seek to understand yourself for the sake of knowledge is part of what it is to be in a loving and respectful relationship with yourself.

As such, self-discovery is the beginning of self-love. How can you create a respectful and loving relationship with yourself if you have no idea where to begin? Professionally, knowing yourself will help you understand when your actions are fully aligned. It allows you to stand behind your ideas fully, the way you are supposed to. In your relationships, self-discovery will enable you to show up fully without losing yourself in the process. It empowers you to draw a line in the sand and back what you believe. You do not compromise your values for clout.

After going through the self-discovery journey, you can evaluate and filter your relationships. Since you know yourself, you can tell whether you are connected with the right people. You will recognize when your new hires, for example, are not the best fit. That way, you can decide where you want to give yourself entirely, and then show up 100% authentically.

The point here is not that you figure out exactly what your perfect life would look like. No one can do that. The point is that living intentionally and being fulfilled demands that you firmly draw lines in the sand and have clear boundaries. Mapping the course guides you in the direction truly meant for you, but taking action requires a commitment to what you know to be right. When you hit a breaking point or reach a defining moment in life, it takes a lot of work to move past it. The techniques in this book are meant to serve as a ladder to help you climb toward the light to the place you truly belong.

The process of self-discovery takes many forms. There are numerous ways to do it, most of which are worth considering. Finding yourself is not a box that you check off a to-do list; it is something you work at every day. Without looking inward, at best, you stay stagnant, and at worst, you become less than you were. On an individual level, self-discovery helps you make more intentional choices. It allows you to find out who you are.

DISCOVER WHO YOU ARE AS A LEADER

Socrates has often been credited with the saying, "Know thyself," but he did not invent it. The motto is inscribed on the frontispiece of the Temple of Delphi. The philosophy, though, still shines through to today. In its imperative form, the assertion shows that man must stand and live by his nature. He must look at himself and find what? And by what means? These are the two questions fundamental to the philosophy. The idea behind the invitation to look within is that knowledge is inherent in man, not outside, and wisdom is learning to remember.

The philosophy deeply holds that when you look within, you will find the answers you are looking for. You will understand what kind of person you are and then figure out how you can live a life that is true to this person. It is a deeply affirming philosophy the truth of which has been echoed through ages.

You have a sort of dialogue between the self and the soul — you ask the questions and answer them. Like Socrates, you question because you do not yet know, and you answer because you can discover the truths you have within. Knowing yourself is the fundamental step to follow. When you figure out what authentic leadership is, which you will in this book, you will be equipped for self-discovery and align your intentions with the things you do. That, in essence, is congruence.

Have you come across people who say one thing and do something else? The world is filled with such people; no wonder the saying "Do as I say, not as I do" is prevalent. Have you, at one point or another, done the same? Have you ever, for example, embellished some aspects of who you are or events to control the way someone saw you? Hopefully, you have grown, or are growing, out of the tendency to do that. Mature people are congruent.

Congruence is about having a sense of consistency between the things you say and do. An incongruent person voices their plans without actually seeing them through. This could be anything from planning to go on a diet and cheating all the time to promising to deliver work on deadline and still missing the deadline.

An incongruent leader requires that people do as they say, not as they do. They act against what they genuinely believe, creating an inauthentic relationship between them and their team.

As a child, what did you make of the person who asked you to emulate their words and not their actions? What about now? What do you think of them? Chances are, you lost respect for the leader who preached one thing and did another. You begin to zone out and stop taking their opinions seriously. They are, to speak plainly, hypocritical. That is what incongruence does. It creates a culture of hypocrisy and threatens all levels of leadership within an organization. Employees begin to believe that transparency and honesty do not matter. They begin to take shortcuts. After all, they can do whatever they want as long as they are not caught. Eventually, your business suffers.

No competent person wants to work for someone who voices their vision and does not follow it up with meaningful action. Real leaders practice what they preach, which can help their teams gain trust in them. They inspire, motivate and speed growth. They act with authenticity and congruence. When they speak, they mean it because they speak from their core values. They do what they say because they say what they really mean.

If you are a leader who tells your team to do something, but your actions contradict your words, you will fail to inspire them. However, when you live according to your values and align your actions with your speech, you deepen your presence. Your energy field becomes palpable. When you enter a room, everything changes just because you are around. Your attention and focus create admiration and respect from others, making a healthy work environment for your team. You fuel their passion for work.

Additionally, when you are in tune with who you are and listen to your intuition, your words are weightier. Those around you know they can take your word to the bank. They are quick to oblige because they believe in you. The congruence that real leaders display instills hope in others and motivates them to go beyond themselves and keep growing. They see that you have mastered yourself and they desire to do the same. They respect your motivation and passion that have allowed you to move beyond your impulses and to delay gratification.

The thing about congruence is that people do not just see it, they feel it. They notice what your presence does to them. They recognize that you are different. Even though increasing revenue is essential, as is improving the bottom line, they know that you are driven by more than that. You do not just focus on profit — you concentrate on yourself. You focus on people.

EIGHT KEY DIMENSIONS OF LEADING FROM WITHIN

Becoming a leader is about having the will to walk a path that builds capacity and competency. This path is not easy or quick to master. There is no silver bullet that leads to confident leadership. Instead, it is about responding to what is needed in a given situation. It is obtaining all the qualities that leaders need in their lives to be true to their name. It is learning to take challenges in a stride and dealing with them without letting them overwhelm you. The path to becoming a leader is one you must walk intentionally, and sometimes, alone.

You will struggle and sometimes you will want to quit. You will work on yourself and repeat the process the next day. You will strive, but in the end, you will reap the benefits. You will win.

In learning the eight key dimensions for leading from within, you will get everything you need to understand the concept of leading from within. These dimensions work together and are all critical. They are like pillars in a building. If one pillar is not firm, even though the others might be, the building is not steadfast. Each of the eight dimensions is discussed in-depth in its own chapter to help you understand them and start working to achieve them. Let's define them first:

Self-awareness

Shelly Duval and Robert Wicklund were the first to define self-awareness in a research capacity. They proposed that people can either focus on their external environment or the self at any one moment. When you focus on yourself, you evaluate and compare your behavior with your internal values and standards. You begin from the things you know to be true for you — core values — and measure how you behave against those. This does not come automatically to most people.

By definition, self-awareness is the ability to focus on who you are and how your emotions, actions, and thoughts align or fail to align with your internal standards. A highly self-aware person can evaluate themselves objectively, manage their emotions, align their behavior with their values, and understand accurately how others see them.

Self-esteem

Self-esteem describes a person's subjective sense of their value or worth. It is how much you appreciate yourself and act lovingly toward who you are even when circumstances are not right. Self-esteem impacts your decisions, emotional health, well-being, and relationships. People with a healthy self-esteem know their skills and are confident in them. They keep good relationships, their expectations of themselves and others are healthy, and they always know their needs and can express them.

Being on Purpose

Purpose often arises from a person's gifts and strengths, setting them apart from others. It is also the basis for a connection with others. True leaders are always on purpose. Being on purpose is about having your life guided by central aims. Your purpose guides your behavior and sense of self while providing meaning to your life. It is unique for everyone and often shifts as you evolve and your priorities in life change.

Authenticity

By definition, authenticity is the quality of being genuine. An authentic person lives their life according to their goals and values rather than by external standards. Authenticity is about being true to your personality, spirit, and values regardless of external pressure to be otherwise. It is about being honest with others and yourself and taking responsibility for your mistakes.

Resilience to Stress

The dictionary defines resilience as the ability to recover quickly from difficulties. Resilience is about adapting well in the face of threats, tragedy, trauma, adversity, or other sources of stress. It is about how you respond to relationship problems, financial stressors, and tension in the workplace. How do you bounce back from difficult experiences? Transformational leaders are resilient to stress.

Empowered Beliefs

Whether they are aware of it, everyone has a belief system or a set of principles that form the basis of how you live. Your belief system can be made of either limiting or empowering beliefs. Limiting beliefs are any beliefs or things that you hold to be true about yourself or the world that do not serve your goal in life. Limiting beliefs stand in the way of progress. A confident leader is one who has learned to overcome their limiting beliefs and embrace empowering ones instead.

Positive Self-talk

Self-talk is your inner dialogue. It is how you talk to yourself and is influenced by your subconscious mind. Your self-talk reveals your beliefs, questions, thoughts, and ideas. Self-talk can either be positive or negative — encouraging or distressing. The confident leader has learned how to harness the power of positive self-talk. They can recognize when their self-talk becomes negative and take the necessary steps to correct that.

Self-love

Self-love is a state of appreciation for oneself. It grows from the actions that support your psychological, spiritual, and physical growth. Self-love means that you have a high regard for your happiness and well-being. It is about taking care of your needs and not sacrificing them for the sake of pleasing others. Self-love means not settling for less than what you deserve, but how it plays out is different for different people and different circumstances.

JUNGIAN ATTITUDINAL FUNCTIONS

Carl Jung, often described as the founder of analytical psychology, was a Swiss psychoanalyst and psychiatrist. His work has influenced religious studies, philosophy, anthropology, psychiatry, literature, and more. His work led to the development of the Myers-Briggs personality test. In his personality theory, he demonstrated how complex the human personality is and the consequences of that complexity. He created different psychological attitudes to explain a person's style of leadership. These attributes affect your personality either positively or negatively, and they influence your ability to lead. These attributes include.

Sensation

It is the process of gathering data directly from sensory organs instead of getting it from the unconscious. Leaders whose personalities lead by the sensing function can develop it to absorb the right information at the right time.

Intuition

Intuition is also referred to as the "know the future" feeling. It is a human personality function that allows people to understand things quickly without consciously reasoning through them. It transmits perceptions unconsciously. A true leader develops their intuition. They simply know the right thing to do and do it. With their self-awareness, experience, and resilience, they can make their choices based on instinct.

Thinking

The thinking function uses reason and logic and focuses less on emotions. The thinking person observes everything around them and thinks about it to further examine what they want to explore. Thinking is the ability to be objective, see things clearly, and use critical reasoning and research to determine the next step.

Feeling

According to Jung, feeling is the process that happens between the ego and the self in any given context. It is not emotions like guilt, sadness, anger, or happiness. As a cognitive function, feeling is about creating an estimation of your surroundings based on values and using that estimate to make decisions.

DIFFERENT TYPES OF TESTS

There are a number of tests that you can take to understand yourself better, including:

1. The MBTI Test (Myers-Briggs Type Indicator)

The MBTI test is an evaluator created by Isabel Briggs and Katherine Briggs Myers. It has been around for over 50 years. It helps you to take an inventory of yourself. You will find out your preferences for decision-making, your source of energy and focus, and how you orient yourself to the outer world. It does not measure intelligence, competence, and skill though. It is based on Jung's theory of personality types but has a few exceptions. Your preferences are reported as either sensing-intuitive, thinking-feeling, extravert-introvert, or judging-perceiving. You will be one of 16 possible combinations of the preferences, but the types are not absolute. If you find that the results do not feel right, reconsider the test because the material is standard and limited only to the 16 types.

2. DiSC or the Personal Profile System (PPS)

The Personal Profile System measures your surface traits. It helps you figure out how you behave in a given environment. It is based on William Moulton Marston's theory of traits model. His theory explains how emotions are responsible for your change in behavior in different situations. The theory behind it is that human behavior can be studied on a bipolar model. It explores your behavior across four traits, including, D —dominance, I — influencing/inducement, S — steadiness/submission, and C — conscientiousness/compliance.

There are four scales within the DiSC system that are represented in a graph using four adjectives to make your profile. There typically are 15 profile patterns, each with a popular pattern of the least and most characteristics. It can help you to improve your communication in the workplace, among other uses.

3. Insights Discovery Profiler

The Insights Discovery test helps you to understand the dynamics between you and how you interact with organizations and teams. It is also based on Jung's work. To take advantage of the framework, you have to understand the relationship between Jung's rational and attitudinal functions. This is typically introduced as four colors — green, yellow, blue, and red — relating to the functions. It explains Jung's preferences to introduce eight main types in the Insights Discovery format.

The system uses a wheel to help you understand and apply the system and to know your related subtypes. You also get a comprehensive personal profile that contains up to 40 pages of information on your strengths, personal style, weaknesses, communication, blind spots, the value you bring to a team, and areas you can develop. There are also sections that cover your management style and personal achievement among other things.

The test is practical and easy to understand. It gives you individual feedback that you can use for personal growth. It also gives you an overview of your organizational strengths and weaknesses when your data is collated with other profiles. This can give you unique insights on how to develop as a leader.

WHO IS A CONFIDENT WIZARD?

Confident leaders have worked on themselves to hone their strengths and fortify their weaknesses. Also known as transformational leaders, they know which core functions to change to become more effective. They do not focus on status or power. They exist to inspire, motivate, and nurture a team of skilled individuals. They do not see themselves primarily as those who possess authority. They see themselves as equals with their employees and provide their support to the team. They accept their employees as they are and work to create strong relationships with them.

The confident wizard never loses sight of their blind spots and is constantly monitoring their thoughts, emotions, and actions. They always make choices and chart their path based on their values, and whenever they have something that needs clarification, they have no qualms about reaching out to their team. Transformational leaders have no problem admitting when they do not know something. They try to improve their skills and those of their team members to create future leaders. They make a space that their employees can share holistically, aware that their employees are "whole human beings". As a result, the environment they create is true to their purposes and passions.

Leaders schedule regular check-ins with team members to find out how they are doing personally and professionally. They champion flexible work policies, allowing their employees to work comfortably and sustainably. They explore ways to support their employees, whether it be providing meditation tools, stocking the office fridge with healthy food choices, or supporting telemedicine appointments. The leader knows that they need the human element in their business and works to keep things that way.

They are in touch with their emotions. They know that a well-rounded leader is someone employees can relate to. Yet, while they are committed to serving others, confident leaders do not neglect self-care. They pay attention to their mental health and recognize when they need to take time to recharge. They have figured out how to incorporate self-care into their routine. That way, they are always prepared to lead the team through whatever comes at them.

SELF-DISCOVERY ACTIVITIES

One way to know that you need to embark on a self-discovery journey is to find out how you wake up. If you find it incredibly difficult to get started on your day, or if some of your leadership responsibilities do not excite you, something is not right. At your very core, you are not satisfied. It could be that some things in your life are not compatible with who you are.

In that case, you would need self-discovery to go back to your authentic self and lead the life you are meant to live. You also need self-discovery if you just want to live a more fulfilling life that is true to your spirit. Self-discovery takes you on an inward journey and helps you rediscover things that once brought you joy that you may have forgotten. The following activities will get you started. Carry them out in one sitting or stretch them across several days as you go about your life.

1. Complete an Association Exercise

Find the right adjective or phrase to complete the following sentences. Do not overthink it; only complete the sentences the way you find them true to you.

- *If I had time, I would ...*
- *My best toy as a child was ...*
- *I have never seen a better movie than ...*
- *My father thinks I should ...*
- *One thing I can never forget is ...*
- *Music that always cheers me up is by ...*
- *I love having ... in my wardrobe.*
- *If I was ... I would believe in myself.*
- *I am most scared of ...*

2. Introspect and Resolve

The first chapter touched on the importance of congruence in a leader. Look at your past and study the times that you have been incongruent. It could be anything from planning to go on a diet, cheating, or failing to keep a deadline. Write down the situation and what you did. Why were you incongruent? How did you feel about it? What did you learn from it? Note two or three instances and identify the trend. List one or two ways you could do better next time.

3. Take a Self-discovery Test

The Insights Discovery Profiler is designed to be a learning experience. It helps you intensely reflect on yourself and creates a safe space to share your aspirations and challenges. After completion, you get an Insights Discovery Personal Profile. The exercise challenges you to reflect on who you are, and from the insights, you can decide how to build your leadership capabilities in authentic ways. The profile gives you an insight into eight critical abilities within the dimensions for leadership and suggests practical ways to enhance your effectiveness in different areas. You will explore your leadership style and use a modular approach to turn your attention to the areas that need further development.

3

BECOME SELF-AWARE

Self-awareness is the conscious knowledge of your feelings and character. When you are self-aware, you can decide where to invest your emotions, energy, and personality to direct the course of your life better. Self-awareness makes you more in tune with your feelings and thoughts, making you more aware of how they guide your life and decisions. It helps you know what makes you tick and how to respond well to others to have more influence, direction, purpose, and success.

Research has shown that self-awareness is one of the most critical skills leaders can develop. Successful leaders know where their natural inclinations lie, and they use this knowledge to either compensate or boost them. They know that the one constant thing in all their interactions and business is themselves, so understanding how they behave is important. They constantly work to understand how their behavior and choices affect others. To them, self-awareness is an ongoing exercise.

The best way to keep developing your self-awareness is to learn to see yourself objectively. This chapter further explores the concept of self-awareness and provides you with techniques and activities to become more self-aware.

QUALITIES OF BECOMING SELF-AWARE

The first quality to becoming self-aware is honesty. As you build it over time, you will begin to see how vital honesty is to becoming a well-rounded and healthy person. Personal growth demands that you commit to taking an honest look at how you act, feel, and think. It means never trying to hide who you are or pretend to be someone else. A true and confident leader does not avoid looking at the areas they need to improve. They work on themselves so that they can live an open and fulfilling life without covering things up. They do not tiptoe around issues, but instead deal with them directly, taking the necessary action to improve themselves in the long term.

Secondly, a true and inspirational leader perseveres. They have the willpower to keep to the course. Perseverance comes from a spirit that refuses to give up. The leader keeps up through technical projects, problems, and amidst confusion. They work regardless of the obstacles, choosing consistency. Inspirational leaders have the stamina to keep to a course of action despite the challenges, disappointment, and discouragement from others. They embody a wide range of skills that empower them to find other solutions where one approach has failed.

Thirdly, a true and inspirational leader is passionate. Passion is a profound feeling for something that is personally and deeply meaningful. It is about vision, and it contains energy, enthusiasm, and excitement. Passion inspires others to identify with and join your course. It is contagious. It elevates productivity and keeps your employees committed to your goals, but to do this, it has to be borne from something significant to you. When you are passionate about a thing, you cannot help but think about it, work on it, and be enthused. Your passion influences what you decide to do every day. It eventually leads to mastery and success, mainly because you always give yourself to your passion.

A true leader's passion is always connected to the hope of making a difference. It may not always be apparent, but when you look closely, the effective leader changes others' lives by their product or through the service they offer.

Finally, a true leader is confident. Confidence is so vital that without it, real leadership cannot exist. Someone may know how to solve problems and communicate better, but "leader" is only a title if they do not believe in themselves. In essence, real leadership demands that you are the first sale. In fact, trying to teach leadership without building self-confidence is like creating a house on sand — no matter how nicely you paint it, it is shaky at best. Confidence allows the leader to take advantage of people's natural tendency to trust confident people.

These four qualities — honesty, perseverance, passion, and confidence — fuel self-awareness. Leaders who have a great sense of self-awareness can understand their limitations. They take responsibility for their weaknesses and commit themselves to be better. Whether it is asking for feedback from their employees or sticking to a self-development program, self-aware leaders are committed to growth.

To be a transformational leader, you must understand who you are as a person, your personality, your strengths, and your weaknesses. This understanding gives you the logical reasoning to know what should be done in the future. As a self-aware individual, you are not afraid of showing your worries, emotions, and drives. You are aware of not just yourself but the environment around you. A self-aware leader can control their impulses, make better decisions, and act accordingly in every situation.

Benefits of Self-awareness

Research by Travis Bradberry and Jean Greaves shows that 83% of self-aware people are top performers and can truly lead. They are not given to making impulsive decisions. Self-aware leaders have learned the value of research, reasoning, and trial-and-error in their personal and professional decision-making. Before listing the benefits, it is essential to discuss the intersection between self-awareness and self-reflection.

In 1979, Lewis theorized that children aged 18 months and above have a level of self-awareness. They understand the concept of the self and can respond to environmental and social cues. While this is part of self-awareness, it is not precisely what is meant in this section. In adults, self-awareness is the capacity to reflect on yourself deeply. It is the ability to learn more about your primary purpose and to introspect willingly.

There are two types of self-reflection. In the first type, you reflect on yourself and constructively try to figure out the best way to hit your targets. In the second type, you attempt to understand and respond to your negative cognitive, behavioral, and emotional reactions. True leaders will use both types of self-reflection. They know that the self-focused approach alone cannot yield much success in goal attainment. The solution-focused approach helps to eliminate rumination and to move you forward toward your goals. That said, the following are the benefits of self-awareness:

Self-awareness boosts creativity and improves relationships.

A self-aware leader is more creative and can lead incredible projects, teams, and assignments. Success is no longer a concept to you, but instead, it is a reality that only time keeps you away from. When self-awareness is used constructively, it improves how you interact with your environment and interpret events which is an aspect of creativity. You are able to solve problems well through perspective-taking.

For social interactions to be effective, you need to understand other people's needs and thoughts as different from theirs. Self-awareness helps with this. It lets you grow in empathy and respond well to the plights of others, improving your connections and relationships.

Self-awareness increases your cognitive function and confidence.

Teams rally behind confident leaders because they can learn from them. Self-awareness improves your confidence by enhancing your self-regulation. You become better at understanding expected social norms and navigating through social triggers like a master. Self-awareness sets you free from the shame you experience when you do not meet social standards. You no longer operate from external drives but have internal standards that trump societal norms. Self-awareness does not do away with social pressures, but it puts them in perspective. It allows you to restrain your social impulses and grow in your personal responsibility to adhere more to your internal standards.

Self-awareness improves your communication skills.

The self-aware person understands what matters to them and the things they can compromise. Since there is clarity in their inner being, they can communicate and negotiate with others better. As a leader, that boosts motivation and productivity. As you grow in self-awareness, how you think about yourself shifts and you begin to see yourself as the cause of success. This mode of being, combined with a robust sense of purpose, makes for a compelling communicator.

The Hawthorne Effect

Research has found that some people tend to work harder and perform better when participating in an experiment or being observed. This is known as the "Hawthorne effect". Under observation, people were found to change their personalities and behaviors. The concept was described for the first time in the 1950s by Henry Landsberger after researching in Hawthorne. At the time, an electric company commissioned research to determine whether there was an interaction between work environments and productivity.

Initially, the study was meant to look at the various elements of the work environments, such as the length of the workday, timings for breaks and lighting, and how they affected the employees' productivity. The researchers conducted many experiments toward that end. In some of them, the focus was to know whether tampering with the amount of light in the workplace would affect worker productivity. It seemed that productivity increased due to the changes but went down after the experiment was complete.

HOW TO ACHIEVE SELF-AWARENESS

Know What You Are Feeling

The practice of naming emotions seems easy at face value, but it can be transformative. Consider this: how often do you lose awareness of how you feel as you work? Most people do not check in on themselves. Knowing how to name your emotions with granularity and specificity will go a long way in improving your self-awareness. The idea is to become emotionally literate. Instead of saying, "I am fine," you delve into the nuances and describe yourself as happy, excited, or enthusiastic.

Note that the idea here is not to label emotions as either negative or positive. No emotion is negative, contrary to popular belief. They are just emotions. What can be negative or positive is how you respond to them. Emotions are messengers. They give you information about something that you could change. Understanding your feelings can help you see them from a different perspective. You can study why you feel as you do and decide how to respond appropriately. The more specific you get, the better you can make a plan to resolve the issue at hand.

Understanding your emotions will protect you from projecting your feelings onto others. It will allow you to communicate better, and as a result, have better relationships with the people you care about. Suppose you get home after a long day at work. If you have low emotional literacy and awareness, you might say that you are in a "bad mood." The ambiguity of the description could leave you helpless and cause you to stew in the unpleasantness, unaware of how you can make your situation better. In not knowing your feelings, you fail to understand your needs, which could cause any number of results, including miscommunication and an argument with your spouse.

Now, consider the same scenario but with an intentional attempt to know what you are feeling. You discover that you feel worried about the status of your project at work. Rather than taking your worry out on your spouse, you ask for alone time to process and decompress. Instead of getting fused with what you are feeling, you gain distance and perspective and act better as a result.

Whether you are feeling strong emotions because you made a mistake, are trying to work through a disagreement or simply want to assert yourself, naming your feelings is a skill you need to cultivate. It reduces anxiety and helps you to control stress. It heightens your self-awareness and equips you to master yourself and avoid patterns of self-sabotage.

Ask For Help

Leaders are not people who do everything that needs doing themselves. You need to be surrounded by people you trust who can help you improve your leadership skills. If you have a team, make a habit of asking them to evaluate your leadership styles. Consider what they want or need in a leader, and it will help you become more self-aware in your practices. Take their comments into account and decide what you will take and what to leave. Determine the parts of yourself that need improvement to better serve others.

Remember that knowing who you are is not an inside job alone. It requires social interaction. It may be scary to ask others for input about yourself, but leadership needs to be divorced from insecurity. Feedback provides a reality check. It is a bit like a guard rail — it ensures that your confidence continues to work for you instead of spilling over into overconfidence. From it, you will see behavior patterns that you did not know you had. Feedback shows you your blind spots. It shows you how your mannerisms, emotions, and communication style affects others.

Know Your Limits

After getting input from others, use that information as a starting place. Figure out how to begin working on yourself, and while you're at it, identify the areas where you excel. It will balance you out as you work on your weaknesses. It will also give you an idea of the things that come easily to you, your skills, and talents to know what you can pass down to your team. What are your strengths and weaknesses? Do you know the areas that you could work on to become a better leader? Should you communicate more? Feedback only helps you if you make it actionable.

Become Mindful

Mindfulness is about bringing awareness to what you are doing, your thoughts, and your opinions. It allows you to accurately communicate your feelings through your demeanor and your perceptions through your tone. Mindfulness helps you order your body language. Being mindful of the way you present yourself to others is a significant step toward self-awareness.

If you find yourself having trouble with mindfulness, keeping a journal will help you look for trends and patterns and see yourself more objectively. Write down what you are feeling and why. It will give you a better understanding of your triggers, emotions, and responses. As a rule of thumb, be honest about what you feel and your reactions.

Keep an Open Mind

Good leaders are, by nature, open and curious about new solutions to problems. They welcome diverse perspectives and ideas, which causes them to grow while making others feel heard, valued, and respected. Being open-minded will go a long way to improving your self-awareness. You will withhold judgment and listen attentively to others' ideas with a sense of curiosity. As a leader, cultivate the skill of accepting others, no matter who they are.

SELF-AWARENESS TECHNIQUES AND ACTIVITIES

So far, it is clear that self-awareness is about having a clear recognition of your overall personality. It is knowing your thoughts, beliefs, weaknesses and strengths, sources of motivation, and emotions. It helps you understand others and how they see you. It is also clear that self-awareness does not come naturally. However, with practice, you can increase your self-knowledge and make the necessary positive changes in your behavior. The activities below will help you get started:

1. Question Journaling

A journal keeps a permanent record of your thoughts and feelings. It provides a place you can look back at in the future and recognize growth. It also allows you to use both the past and present as opportunities to learn. Set aside some time to answer the questions below in your journal. It will help you to understand yourself better. You can journal on paper or your laptop, provided you answer the questions honestly and with some introspection.

On Your Past

- *What three experiences shaped who you are? How did they do this?*
- *If you could change something in your past, what would it be?*

On Your Present

- *Describe yourself in one paragraph.*
- *Does your personality resemble any of your parents?*
- *What is your biggest strength? What is your biggest weakness?*

On Your Future

- *Describe your ideal "you."*
- *What is keeping you from your goals?*
- *How much time do you give to the most essential things in your life?*

2. Practice Mindfulness Meditation

Mindfulness meditation is an awareness that you raise by focusing on the moment without judgment. It teaches you to stay present. The process is simple:

- Find a quiet place without any disturbances and

sit comfortably — it could be on the floor or a chair. Keep your neck and back straight.

- Keep your focus on the present. Focus on your breath. How does the air you are breathing in feel? Notice how your body is responding to it. Notice the differences between each breath — breath in through your nose and out through your mouth.
- Notice each thought that enters your mind. If you are worried, notice it, and leave it be. Do not ignore your thoughts, simply acknowledge them, and anchor yourself through your breath.
- If your mind keeps wandering, do not be too hard on yourself. Try again by bringing your focus back to your breath. Initially, you can do this exercise for a minute, but you can do it for longer as you get more familiar.

3. Practice Grounding Techniques

Research has shown that grounding can help people calm down quickly. It is an excellent technique to develop self-awareness. Grounding brings you into the moment, the way mindfulness does. To get started, you can use the "Grounding Chair" technique. You can use it outside and barefoot.

- Sit on a comfortable seat where your feet can

touch the ground and close your eyes. Begin
breathing in and out after three counts.

- Focus on your body and notice how it feels.
  How do your feet and legs feel? What about
  your back pressed against the chair? Notice the
  feel of the seat's fabric.
- Next, imagine your feet pressing into the
  ground. Picture your energy draining from
  your mind down through your feet and into the
  ground. As the energy drains, notice the way
  each part feels, then relax your muscles. Feel the
  sense of heaviness leaving your body into the
  ground.

4

RAISE YOUR SELF-ESTEEM

A person with healthy self-esteem is assertive in expressing what they think and letting others know their needs. They are confident in their decision-making and realistic in their expectations, which means that they are not overly critical. People with high self-esteem are resilient, better able to deal with setbacks, and handle stress well. This is because self-esteem affects every facet of your life. When you know your worth and have good self-esteem, you feel worthwhile and secure. You generally develop positive relations with other people and are confident in your abilities. You become open to feedback and learning new things which helps you gain and master new skills.

Low self-esteem is a contagious thing — anyone can be inflicted. Have you ever been in a position where you did well, but then refused to acknowledge that success because you wondered whether you really deserved it? It can affect you and anyone around you. Someone could be covering up their low self-esteem by being the loudest in the room. On the other hand, a timid person could be so because they are suffering from low self-esteem. Unless you know what to look for in your behaviors, you can assume that you have healthy self-esteem, while the opposite is true.

A leader with high self-esteem is not threatened by others' ideas. They have no problem encouraging others to be their best. On the other hand, a leader with low self-esteem is controlling, discouraging, and often micromanaging. They often take credit for the work others put in. To them, people exist only to prop them up. This chapter highlights why self-esteem is important, and what a leader can do to build their self-esteem.

WHAT IS SELF-ESTEEM?

Self-esteem is the way you think about yourself. It is your overall sense of worth or value and can be considered a measure of how much you appreciate, approve of, and like yourself (Stewart, 2004). Other researchers describe self-esteem as a person's attitude toward themselves. Seen that way, it can be "good" or "bad."

Factors such as health, age, personality, genetics, social circumstances, life experiences, and so forth are believed to influence self-esteem. Perhaps the most important thing to note about self-esteem, as per research, is that it is not fixed. It is measurable and malleable, and you can improve on it.

Psychologists have been talking about self-esteem for decades, going back and forth on it. The founding father of psychology, Sigmund Freud, had theories about self-esteem. He suggested how it develops and what influences it, and psychologists have been working on that since. Over the years, they have narrowed down what constitutes self-esteem and what sets it apart from other self-directed characteristics. For the sake of clarity, we will discuss a few of those distinctions before digging into how you can develop self-esteem.

First, self-esteem differs from self-concept. It is a part of it. The self-concept is how you perceive yourself. It is the answer to "Who am I?". It is about knowing your tendencies, hobbies, thoughts, and habits. Self-esteem is part of the awareness of who you are. Secondly, self-esteem is not the same as self-image. Self-image resembles self-concept because it is about your perception of yourself, but self-image is not based on reality. It is based on subjective thoughts and feelings. As such, a person's self-image could be close to reality — or it could be far from it. Thirdly, even though self-esteem is similar to self-worth, there are slight differences. Self-esteem is what you think, believe, and feel about yourself, while self-worth is a global acknowledgment that we are human and that to be human is to be worthy of love.

It is important to note that while self-esteem is inevitably tied to self-confidence, they are not the same. Self-confidence is about how you trust yourself and your abilities to solve problems, deal with issues, and engage well with the world. Self-confidence is based on external measures for value and success, while self-esteem is based on internal measures. This means that it is possible to have high self-confidence in one area but still lack a high overall sense of value or self-esteem. Self-esteem is mostly tested in how you respond to failure. A self-confident person may believe that they can write a report well, but if it is criticized, and if they have low self-esteem, they lose their confidence in their abilities.

Similarly, self-efficacy and self-esteem are connected, but they are not the same. Self-efficacy is about believing that you can succeed in given tasks. You could have a high self-efficacy when succeeding in a management training program but have low self-efficacy regarding leading the whole organization. Self-efficacy is more specific and is based on external measures of success.

Finally, self-esteem is not the same as self-compassion. Self-compassion is about the way you relate to yourself instead of how you perceive yourself. If you are self-compassionate, you are forgiving and kind, and you avoid being harsh. Self-compassion can cause healthy self-esteem, but it is not self-esteem. In the techniques and practices to increase self-esteem, you will notice how these concepts intertwine more specifically, but one way to conceptualize the value of self-esteem is to think about Maslow's hierarchy of needs.

Esteem is on the fourth level of the hierarchy. Maslow's esteem needs, though, are focused on external measures like recognition, respect, prestige, and accomplishment. These are only a small component of self-esteem. The confident leader has to grow and nourish their need for inner respect before working on external measures. They have to figure out who they are, the things that shaped them, and how they can act consistently across time. The confident leader must master themselves before they can begin to rule the world.

Simply put, building your self-esteem is not about projecting or having an image of confidence. It is about being truly confident. It is not about external behaviors that you have to show — looking sharp, walking upright, and maintaining eye contact when in conversation. It is about internal attributes that give birth to certain external behaviors.

There are specific characteristics connected with having high self-esteem, such as being open to criticism, receiving compliments, and acknowledging mistakes. People with high self-esteem do not shy away from showing their curiosity and discussing their ideas and opportunities. They can dig deep and tap into their inner creativity. They have loving and respectful relationships because they appreciate themselves and others. They are always looking to make a difference in the lives of others.

Based on these traits, you can come up with examples of high self-esteem at work. Imagine a well-performing student who takes an exam and fails. He may explain his failure as not studying comprehensively or that it was an especially difficult exam. He does not conclude that he is stupid and likely to fail other tests in the future. Healthy self-esteem guides him to accept his reality, think critically about failure, and begin solving the problem rather than give up or wallow in self-pity.

Alternatively, think about a young man going on a first date with a young woman he likes. Eager to impress and connect with her, he ends up talking for a good chunk of the first half-hour. Somehow, he course-corrects, and as they talk, he realizes that she is driven by values that differ entirely from his. They do not have much in common. Rather than agreeing with her opinions, he gives his and is not afraid to disagree with her. Because of his high self-esteem, he stays true to his values, which helps him communicate well even when not in agreement. To him, the most critical thing is to live authentically rather than focus on winning his date's approval.

If you love and believe that you can do anything you put your mind to, you have high self-esteem. Leaders should be confident about their abilities and their value. In loving yourself for who you are, you can take challenges and deal with them well. As a thing to note, building your self-awareness will build your self-esteem. It will guide you through life with your head held up high. This does not mean that you will never have to deal with doubt. It is human to doubt yourself once in a while. With high self-esteem, you can deal with doubt well and soar to new heights, making you a prominent transformational leader. How, then, do you build your self-esteem?

HOW TO GAIN SELF-ESTEEM

Practice Self-compassion; Be Kind to Yourself

Love comes easy on the good days. It is when you fail that your kindness to yourself suddenly wanes. You begin to dwell on your faults, and your internal monologue keeps going with harsh judgments. You begin to shame and blame yourself for your pain and make a habit of abandoning yourself for whatever would comfort you. Self-compassion is a way to reclaim your heart. It is about treating yourself with care and kindness like you would a friend.

Self-kindness is acting in understanding ways toward yourself rather than being critical. For the self-compassionate, their inner voice is warm and supportive. They recognize that everyone has weaknesses, which gives them a sense of inclusivity instead of alienation. Instead of becoming self-critical, self-compassion turns you gently toward self-care. Rather than listening to the voice inside you telling you that you can't do it, you challenge it, prove it wrong, and flip it around.

The same way you ask a struggling friend what they need is how you can answer that question. When you sense yourself becoming self-critical, pause, and ask yourself, "What do I need?". If you cannot answer, find ways in which you already care for yourself and do your best to incorporate them into your life when you are having difficulties. Always treat yourself like a friend you care about — nurture yourself, soothe your feelings, validate them, and then motivate yourself to act. Each situation will demand different ways to be compassionate with yourself but always say "no" to the voice inside telling you that things are impossible.

Explore Where Your Beliefs Come from

Have you ever considered why you believe the things that you do? Where do your beliefs come from? Have you ever considered how they got there? Was the process intentional? Did you consciously choose to be a certain way, or did you simply wake up as you are? Are you even aware of your beliefs? Do they exist independently from your conscious self? Did you adopt them from someone you admire, such as parents or friends? Do they propel you toward greatness or do they keep you trapped in monotony and misery? Do you serve them, or do they serve you? Who is in charge?

There are things that we know to be true, like the color of the sky, and then there are things that we wish were true. When we believe something for long, we form an emotional attachment to it. The belief becomes familiar, safe, and comfortable. It brings a level of certainty and predictability to our lives. This is because the things we believe shape us — for most people, anyway.

For others, the things they believe are because of who they are — they shape what they believe. To excel as a leader and build your self-esteem, you cannot live by conforming to pre-existing beliefs. You cannot live out a script for life that you did not write. You have to examine your beliefs.

There are different types of beliefs. Positive ones help you to stay productive, empowered, positive, and creative. They allow you to explore and live out your potential. They push you through the uncomfortable seasons of life and allow you to handle your fears, coming out stronger, and wiser. Negative beliefs destroy your potential, happiness, mental health, and relationships if you let them. There are also incidental beliefs that are typically not life-changing. For example, if you believe that the sun will rise tomorrow, it does not change who you are.

To build your self-esteem, look back to your past and understand what has made you the person you are. Do you love to help people in need? Find out why that is. Explore the events that happened in your life that birthed the things that you believe and value.

Have a Talk with Yourself

Sometimes, the things stopping you are things only you can identify. To do this, you have to cultivate openness and identify your default rules and beliefs. For example, what thoughts run through your head in the minutes leading up to a big decision? What automatic explanations do you give for a mistake you've made? Call yourself to a meeting and have this conversation. If the idea of a meeting with yourself sounds odd, you can use a confidence journal. Create a routine that will help you be aware of the things influencing your behavior, your expectations, and their degree of influence.

Try to figure out what is stopping you from becoming as confident as you would like to be. It could be anything from a statement you once heard about confident people to a fear of how others would perceive you. Discover what you say about yourself and find out exactly what it is that you want. If your self-talk is negative, you will have difficulties building confidence. Negative self-talk could include telling yourself how weak you are or criticizing yourself. Challenge those harsh words. They could be the reason you are having difficulties becoming a better person.

Learn to Let Go

Holding on to the past fixes nothing. Replaying it repeatedly or wishing that things had gone differently changes nothing. When it comes to the past, the best approach is to accept what you are holding on to and then let go. That is the way to change things — you have to release whatever is holding you back, even if that feels impossible. Holding on to something from the past stops you from cultivating a strong sense of identity, and it stands in the way of healthy self-esteem. The unpleasant emotions soon become part of your identity, messing up with even more parts of your life.

As you talk with yourself, find out the things that cause you to judge yourself. What is it about your conduct in the past that seems so unforgivable? Try to put the finger on your resentments against yourself. They could be stopping you from becoming a confident leader. Once you identify them, acknowledge them, and then let them go. The act of letting things go is pushing away the thoughts you have about yourself that do not serve your goals, then replacing them with positive affirmations.

Accept That Everyone Makes Mistakes

Mistakes are life's way of teaching us lessons, and sometimes, they are hard to deal with. Yet, it does not come naturally to think of mistakes as lessons. How do you deal with yourself when you stumble and fall? We make mistakes often, but the important thing is that we dust ourselves off and move forward. A mistake is like a momentary lapse in judgment. Everyone makes them. It may not seem like this is true in the moments of the hurt that come from the mistake, but you can begin setting yourself up for it by accepting that mistakes are simply a part of life.

If you are to build your self-esteem, do not beat yourself up for making a mistake. It is not something you can change. Instead, learn from it and move forward. Learn to forgive yourself for past errors. It will allow you to see the future clearly. The point here is not that you shouldn't feel bad for making a mistake. You can mourn a mistake without letting it define you. It is looking past your mistake that will help you define your tomorrow as a better person. It is how you fix the mistake.

As a general principle, always strive to be the best version of yourself, but when you fall short of perfection, as you often will, accept that. Remind yourself that everyone has been there, then focus on the things that you can change. Train yourself not to get hung up on things that you cannot control; otherwise, you will not do much in life. Focus your energies on doing the things that you actually can do.

Find Out Who You Are

To truly know who you are is the most essential skill anyone can ever have. When you know yourself, you know the things that you have to do. You no longer need to ask for permission to do what you ought.

Knowing yourself allows you to escape the frustration caused by giving your energies to the wrong things. It shows you the best places to invest your efforts. Once you know yourself, you become more confident. You understand what you are about and can begin making an impact in the world.

As you talk with yourself, find out what you really want in life. If you could have the best life possible for yourself, what would it look like? Answering this question will give you a sense of purpose, which can triple your self-esteem. From there, allow yourself to make only the choices that serve your purpose. Do what makes you happy, and you will think positively. You will become proud of yourself, grow your confidence, and develop a new sense of self-worth.

ACTIVITIES TO GAIN SELF-ESTEEM

So far, it is clear that building your self-esteem will change your world. It helps you escape from the trap of overvaluing what you are not and undervaluing what you are. Self-esteem will get you into the real action of becoming who you really are inside. The following five techniques will help to get you started.

1. Empty the Envy-meter

Whether you are comparing how you look with someone's Instagram profile or comparing your salary with what your friends make, it is not healthy to make comparisons. Research has found that envy is directly linked with self-esteem. People who compare themselves to others feel worse about themselves. If you catch yourself envying another person's life, remind yourself of the areas you have succeeded and of your strengths. Keep a gratitude journal if you must. It will help you focus on your life rather than others'. It will remind you that you are your own competition. Everyone is in a different race, so there is no need to measure each other by one finish line.

2. Check Your Friends

The people you interact with regularly hugely influence your self-esteem. As an exercise, look at who you spend most of your time with and assess how they make you feel. Do they bring you down or lift you up? Are your friends accepting or constantly judging? Do they respect you and your choices? Surround yourself with people whose attitudes and thoughts you would not mind adopting. If you feel bad about yourself after spending time with person X, it might be time to end the relationship. You want your friends to want what is best for you.

3. Practice Self-care

It is hard to love yourself if you are constantly abusing your body. Conversely, if you make a habit of caring for yourself, you know that you are loving your spirit, body, and mind, and so you feel confident. Watch what you eat. Food has many benefits, including building your self-confidence and self-esteem. Fuel your body with healthy foods, and you will feel more energized, healthier, and better about yourself. Secondly, incorporate exercise into your routine. Research has proven that physical activity boosts confidence. Regular physical activity will boost your body image, which will cause you to feel more confident. Think about your eating habits and exercise and make the relevant changes to your lifestyle.

4. Practice Positive Self-talk

How you talk to yourself inevitably affects how you see yourself. You can use self-talk to build self-compassion and deal with the doubt associated with new challenges. Ask yourself how you would want your friends to talk about you. Would you love it if they defined you as kind and supportive? Whatever it is, figure it out. Then, the next time you start to feel afraid of speaking up or face an obstacle, remind yourself that your thoughts do not always capture reality. Instead of telling yourself things like "I can't take this," say to yourself, "I have to try". Reframe your thoughts to think more positively.

5. Face Your Fears One by One

What things have you been putting off? Maybe you have been waiting to feel more confident before you apply for a promotion. Identify one fear and face it. The best way to build your confidence is to face your fear head-on. To start with, only face the fear you want to address. If you are afraid of speaking up because you fear being embarrassed, speak up anyway. Each time you do, you will gain more confidence which will help you take the next risk.

5

FIND YOUR PURPOSE

E very person's life is directed by their central motivating aims. Purpose guides life decisions and influences behavior. It shapes goals, gives a sense of meaning, and provides direction. For some people, purpose is connected to their vocation. For others, purpose is found in their responsibilities to their family. It is unique for everyone. When you know that your path may be different from other people's and understand why you are on this earth, you can work alongside that to live a meaningful life.

Being on purpose means living a life that is driven by purpose. The dictionary defines purpose as the reason for which something exists. If you are on purpose, you are aligned with why you exist. This definition only covers part of it. It suggests that knowing your purpose is knowing what you are meant to do — and what you want to do with your life. This knowledge can help you plan for your future. It can help you set up a team of like-minded individuals who can help you live out your purpose as you serve the same in their lives. Jack Hawley defined purpose as the place within where our values, talents, and service-drive stay. It is always there, but it is possible to be too busy to notice it.

Imagine someone who keeps doing a job they once loved. After years of toiling, they realize that they no longer find joy in any of the tasks they do every day. They then have to go back to the drawing board, find themselves, and re-align to their purpose. Purpose is such that it can be overshadowed by the daily mundane. You can get so caught up with doing what you need to do every day until you lose sight of what matters to you. Yet, it does not always have to be so.

When you finally uncover your purpose, your attitude to your work changes, your creativity returns, and you perform better at whatever you do. It permeates your whole life, and nearly everyone in your life sees it. This is because purpose is much larger than any goals you have set. This chapter provides insights into why finding your purpose in life is an important thing. It goes into detail on how a future leader can know their purpose and how they can manifest it into a proper leadership role.

BEING ON PURPOSE

A purpose-driven life is so focused that it could be confused with obsessiveness toward something. Purpose releases energy so that the higher it is, the more energy it produces. The deeper your sense of purpose, the freer you feel. You become more open to the possibilities, which is what sets purpose apart from obsessiveness. Obsession is draining, but purpose strengthens. It increases your joy; it does not take away from it. Passionate and focused people have a sense of fulfillment that an obsessive person does not have.

You probably have listened to someone being interviewed about what they do, and their answer was "I was meant to do it." Such phrasing often makes it seem as if some people were meant to achieve just one goal in their life. What happens when the goal is achieved? Does that mean that you no longer have a purpose? Purpose is not about a career. It is the natural flow of your gifts and strengths as they serve those you interact with. The way it manifests depends on how you can tap into it and the circumstances you are facing at the moment. Purpose is constant, but how you manifest it changes with situations.

One researcher described purpose as the flow that lifts and charts the course of one's life on an elevated level. It is intrinsically rewarding, and it justifies life in the present moment instead of always being held captive to a possible gain in the future. Leaders who live on purpose infuse that sense of purpose and their energy into their work and infect those around them with it. They are always orbiting around their purpose no matter what they do.

It is important to note that no one always has their purpose all figured out. Part of being on purpose is the endless journey of exploration. The core remains the same, but as one moves through their life, their reality changes, and their clarity increases or decreases depending on their decisions. Leaders dedicate themselves to heightening their awareness of their purpose after discovering it. Think of it like orbiting around a planet and focusing on an image slowly. Over time, you develop core talents that serve your core values. Whenever they show up, your leadership is transformative and inspiring.

As a general principle, finding your purpose may not be a one-time event. It may demand that you dedicate yourself to clarifying your core values slowly. The activities provided later in this chapter are meant to make your journey smoother, not to eliminate it. Sometimes, it will come to you in the form of insight in a quiet moment. Other times, it will be an energetic vitality you experience when doing some tasks. You may have glimpses of it while doing different things, and often it will not be things that you expect. But when it happens, the insight is clear, and it connects with significant experiences in your life.

Ask yourself what your end goal is. What is it that you hope to achieve with your life? How do you hope to meet this goal? A leader creates several smaller goals that help them achieve their bigger purpose. When those goals are done, they still have a purpose to work and fight for because you can never exhaust purpose. Goals come and go as you move up in the world, but purpose remains. When a leader stays on purpose, their team is inspired. Your team works to become like you, and they collaborate with you to achieve similar goals.

When you understand purpose, all the challenging experiences in life become part of a larger meaning. They serve to forge your character, identity, and meaning. They take on the role of a teacher and you become the willing student. For a person without a purpose, their circumstances dominate their awareness and take over their reason for existing. Their life loses connection with meaning. They simply go with the flow, as though things just happen to them. The person without purpose tends to play the victim when they encounter problems. When you understand purpose, you will have agency. You will operate from a knowledge that you are capable of adapting and responding to circumstances of change. Things do not simply happen to you.

In a sense, purpose is your spirit seeking to be expressed. It is one of the most useful and practical ways to live and lead transformatively. It converts average-performing people to highly spirited and effective workers. With purpose, you not only become a leader in an organization, but you also lead in life. This is because your purpose is how you contribute to humanity.

Some people hesitate about pursuing their life purpose. They fear that they will be embarking on a self-serving quest. However, purpose is truly about recognizing your gifts and taking advantage of them as you strive to make the world better. It is using them to make those around you better. True purpose ends all selfish decisions.

Finally, it is worth noting that questions about purpose could arise at different times in your life, even though they tend to be prevalent at a time of crisis. As you grow to different phases in life, you may begin to feel cramped, and your spirit will demand that you expand to accommodate the growth. New possibilities come up, and if you let it, your purpose evolves. The secret to always being on purpose is to reframe your questions about life repeatedly.

BENEFITS OF BEING ON PURPOSE

Living on purpose feels clear, alive, and authentic. You are likely to experience "flow," which is a state of being fully absorbed in whatever you are doing. Time appears to disappear, and you feel fulfilled and content. Purpose has numerous psychological and emotional benefits. A study conducted in 2010 found that people with a sense of purpose felt a sense of control and were more likely to think of life as worthwhile. Research has also linked a sense of purpose with health outcomes like fewer heart attacks and better sleep. The following are the known benefits of having a sense of purpose:

- **Longer Life** – A study involving 73,000 Japanese women and men found that those who had connected with their sense of purpose lived longer.
- **Protection against Heart Diseases** – Another study associated a lack of purpose with cardiovascular disease and death.
- **Preventing Alzheimer's Disease** – Research on thousands of elderly subjects found that

those with a low sense of purpose were over two times more likely to develop Alzheimer's.

- **Better Pain Management** – Women with a sense of purpose were found to better withstand cold and hot stimuli on their skin.
- **Better Relationships** – A study involving 1,000 adults found that those with a sense of meaning spend more attention and time on their loved ones. People with a sense of purpose are more engaged with their neighbors, friends, and families, creating satisfying relationships.
- **Improved Resilience** – People with purpose can find meaning in the things that happen to them. They can reappraise situations and regulate their emotions, turning unfortunate events into opportunities.

HOW TO FIND YOUR PURPOSE

Most people have no clue what they want with their life. They finish school, get a job, make money, and move to the next stage in life without giving it much thought. If you would like to live a life of purpose, ask yourself the following five questions to find your purpose.

What is your passion?

Take some time alone and write down the things you want most in life. Ask yourself what your passion is to figure things out. List everything that comes to mind first, then rule out what is not at the core. If it is on the list and you realize that you would still consider yourself to have lived well if you never did it, strike it out. It could be that you want to end world hunger. Perhaps you want to create the next big tech idea and serve the world that way. Whatever it is, figure it out. Finding your passion will help you to plan the rest of your goals accordingly.

What are your talents?

On another piece of paper, write down the things you are good at. Like with the first question, list everything that comes to mind, however unconnected they might seem. Whether it is organization, communication, or dancing, write anything you see fit without judgment. By determining your capabilities, you can find out what your purpose should look like and figure out what you would find worth living for.

What do you value?

Earlier, we discussed why values matter for the transformational leader. Now you can take the time to find what your core values are. Do you value adventure? Do you value respect? Figuring out your core values will help you to become well-rounded as a leader. You will be able to pick a productive team that embodies the same values that you hold dear.

What are your inner convictions?

Take some time to get in touch with your inner self. What do you want? What do you believe in? As you explore this question, it pays to ask yourself what you would do if money — or whatever else you feel is limiting you — were of no consequence. Figuring out your inner convictions will help you to project them with integrity and confidence.

Do you know your inner saboteur?

While it is not always obvious, sometimes we can be our worst enemy. There is always a voice inside that tries to sabotage the things we are trying to do. If it has gone unchecked for a while, it could be sabotaging you in small and unnoticeable ways. It pays to listen to that voice and intentionally silence it. You do this by identifying the ways you may be self-sabotaging and your limiting beliefs. Why are you doing things that harm your overarching goal?

Do you suffer from Impostor Syndrome?

Imposter Syndrome refers to the belief that you are not as competent in what you are doing as other people. It is the experience of feeling like a fake. Have you ever experienced Imposter Syndrome? How often do you have to deal with it? What is your go-to response when you catch yourself feeling like a phony?

It is not enough to answer these questions in detail and honestly. You also need to follow through with action. The most hated leaders are incongruent people. They say one thing yet do another. These leaders tell their employees to do something that they would not even attempt. In a sense, they encourage others to copy their words, not their actions, which creates an unbalanced relationship. Transformational leaders stay true to their words. They live by their beliefs. Your purpose can help you to create this in yourself.

ACTIVITIES FOR FINDING YOUR PURPOSE

You cannot find and live a purposeful life without contemplation and activation. Contemplation is about finding the answers to questions about who you are, where you belong, and how you should live life. Activation is about letting go of the judgments and expectations of others and staying in the moment to live out the answers you find in your contemplative practices. The following five exercises will help you with these two aspects toward finding and being on purpose:

1. Find Your *Ikigai*

Ikigai is Japanese for "reason for life." It is the common ground between the things you love, what you excel at, what the world needs, and what you could get paid to do. It is about answering the following questions:

- *What am I good at?*
- *What is my job?*
- *What does the world need from me?*
- *What do I love?*

Work toward your *ikigai* with time, and you will continue to grow and develop. Write the questions, each in a circle, and list the answers for each in its circle. Next, find connections between the circles. For example, if you love something that the world needs, the two circles cross. When you feel that you understand yourself adequately, brainstorm on things that could be your *ikigai*. How do all four aspects intersect? Figure out what you need to start doing and begin right away.

2. Take a Bold Action

You cannot begin being on purpose without doing something. What you do is the difference between where you are and where you want to go. Once you know your *ikigai*, think about where you would like to be next year. Break down that goal into several concrete changes you can make. Grab a calendar and assign one action for each month for the next year. Focus only on one area per month to make sure that your goal is manageable.

3. Question Journaling

Set aside and answer the following questions in your journal as honestly as you can:

- *If you did not have a job, how would you spend your days?*
- *What makes you lose track of time?*
- *What things do you keep close to your heart?*
- *What conversations do you enjoy having with your dearest friends?*
- *What is on your bucket list?*

4. Pay Attention to Your Dreams

Dreams are a way for your unconscious to deal with issues you may not yet be conscious of. While not all dreams are prophetic, dreams can give you accurate insights into your needs, concerns, and desires. They are highly symbolic. Set an intention to remember what you dream and keep a dream journal. Allow yourself a few minutes every morning to write what you remember. You will start to remember more as you keep practicing. Do not concern yourself with interpreting the dreams at first, only recording them. No matter how irrational the dream seems, write it down without editing it. Note the words used in the dream, where you are, how you felt, and so forth. Allow the meaning to emerge on its own.

6

FIND YOUR AUTHENTIC SELF

Being authentic feels amazing — it is empowering, freeing, and liberating. But working to uncover your authentic self can feel monumental and daunting. Philosophers, scientists, artists, and spiritualists have battled with "Who am I?" for millennia. Answering it is a life-long process, but it does not have to be difficult.

To be an authentic leader, there are some things you need to determine first. Your authentic self is an expression of your core needs, beliefs, desires, emotions, traits, and thoughts. It is the person you would be and the behavior you would display if you were not afraid of the negative consequences of your actions. So, the first question to ask is "How real am I?". For many people, the message to "be yourself" feels difficult and impractical. One of the ways to demystify it is to understand the concept of authenticity in depth. Figure out the behavioral dimensions where you can tangibly and visibly showcase your authenticity, then find out if you are doing that.

Once you understand the different aspects of authenticity, ask yourself how you show up in them. When you interact with others, is the experience real or fake? Pinpoint what aspects constitute your authentic self, then live in them more often. When you are interacting with others, do you show your true colors or are you hiding some of your traits so you can fit in? There are different ways — consciously or not — that people hide parts of themselves to be accepted.

In some cases, people might fail to express their emotions. They may hide their anger, disgust, or fear because they worry that the emotions are not acceptable. In other cases, you may hide your happiness or surprise. You do this in the way you communicate, either verbally or nonverbally. The magic, though, happens when you have a clear understanding of how you want to behave across different dimensions and what would constitute your authentic self. Exploring that gives you clues that help you to show up authentically more often. This chapter talks about authenticity and defines it. You will get an in-depth knowledge of what an authentic leader can do and how to achieve this sense of authenticity.

WHAT DOES AUTHENTICITY MEAN?

The authentic leader focuses on projecting who they really are and the things they truly believe in. In today's world, many influencers seem nice when they are in the eyes of their followers, but the situation is different when they are not under watch. Some are cruel and inconsiderate to their employees. No leader who deserves the title should live like that. A true leader does not have inauthentic sides to their personality. Here, it is worth noting that inauthentic people do not follow the true definition of a transformational leader.

If you have two sides to your personality, it means that you still have some work to do on yourself. The authentic leader does not have a personality for work and another one for their home. They do not try to come across differently in front of their colleagues than their managers. Even when they are under pressure to match their personality to their role, they do not yield. Authenticity in leadership is not about playing the role of the leader. It is about being the leader. At the very basic level, authenticity is about being genuine, and not a copycat. It implies embodying your true self in your role as a leader. It means drawing on your principles, values, beliefs, and morals to create a guiding compass in your job. You use your compass, not someone else's.

Contrary to what many people assume, authentic leadership is not about copying the traits and styles of other leaders, even though you can learn from them. It is about showing the behaviors drawn from who you really are at all times. As such, you need a high level of self-awareness. You need to know what you will allow in your life and what is a no-no. Authentic leadership is at heart, from the heart. It flows from your essence and manifests as characteristics that others can respect, back, and aspire toward.

An authentic leader is focused on the result. They work to show their team their true personality. The hope is to inspire the people you lead to be themselves and improve their skills. An authentic leader is not about what everyone else is doing. They do not simply go with the flow or follow fads, even though some have been proven successful. They know from within what matters, and they give themselves to that.

When you are an authentic leader, you follow your heart. You pursue things you have a never-ending passion for, meaning that you are here for the long term. Authentic leaders have a passionate goal. They work toward that goal for their whole lives. Of course, this is not about making more money or creating another team. It is about creating relationships that last a lifetime with people who want to help you achieve your goals and dreams.

QUALITIES OF AN AUTHENTIC LEADER

The key component of authenticity in leadership is genuineness, but there are several markers that authentic leaders share. For example, they live in a way that enables others to trust them all the time. They take responsibility for their actions and are not afraid to own their mistakes. Below are some of the qualities authentic leaders have.

Genuine and Self-aware

Authentic leaders know their emotions, strengths, and limitations. They show their team their real selves. They do not hide their weaknesses out of fear that they would look weak. Instead, they accept that they, too, are a work in progress.

Mission-driven

Authentic leaders know how to put the goals and missions of their organizations ahead of their self-interests. Their work is not about ego, money, or power. Instead, they work from a genuine desire to see goals achieved and help people.

Lead with the Heart

Authentic leaders do not just use their minds in their leadership. They let others see their vulnerability and emotions. They communicate directly and with empathy, which helps them to connect with their employees.

Do Not Lose Sight of the Long Term

In their leadership, authentic leaders do not just keep their eyes on the tasks at hand. They know how everything contributes to the big picture. Their approach to life and choices is that it yields results in the moment and across time.

To embody these traits, the authentic leader keeps their commitment to continuous learning to understand themselves and others around them. They do not work from their ego — they know that if they work from the heart, they can truly empower others. Bear in mind that there is no model leader. Each authentic leader has a unique combination of the skills, traits, styles, and characteristics that constitute authenticity. The goal of this section is not to have you copy these traits but to find them within yourself and nurture them in alignment with who you really are.

In that sense, you can think of authenticity as the alignment of your head, heart, mouth, and feet. It is the consistency across what you are feeling, saying, thinking, and doing. That builds trust and inspires people.

HOW TO GAIN AUTHENTICITY

Discovering your authentic style of leadership will require courage and honesty. You must reflect on your experiences, own your story, and understand your motives and values. The good thing about leading with authenticity is that it is worth it. It will create a balance in your life, create trust in others, and empower them to be authentic. It will have a lasting impact. How, then, do you develop your sense of authenticity? How do you stay true to who you are when there is pressure to be a certain way? How do you understand yourself enough to trust the wisdom in your value system?

1. Know Your Limits

Knowing your strengths and weaknesses will help you show up authentically to your team. When you do the self-analysis to know what you are good at, you can understand where to invest your energies. You will know when to communicate your concerns. Your weaknesses are no longer a blind spot. You can begin working on them. In understanding your limits, you create a well-defined team that will soon grow to trust your leadership capabilities.

2. Listen and Be Open to Feedback

A leader is comfortable with the fact that a team member may be better than them at something. They are open-minded. A transformational leader is not afraid to accept constructive criticism from their team. It displays confidence in the team's abilities, builds team pride, and creates a nurturing environment for everyone to work in.

3. Practice Emotional Intelligence

Emotional intelligence is about understanding who you are, managing your emotions, and understanding other people's reactions to build strong relationships. Everyone responds differently to situations. Some follow their impulses, creating unprofessional outbursts of anger. The authentic leader understands why they need a calm mind. They respond to situations with integrity and pride. The world does not end simply because something bad has happened. A true leader knows this and keeps their emotions in check. They solve challenges with proper reasoning and logic.

When you know how to deal with your emotions, it is easier to share your concerns with your team. It helps you show up with your feelings and thoughts well processed. This means that you can build good relationships with your team.

4. Be Mindful

Take the time to be quiet and on your own. Observe your thoughts and understand them. Mindfulness helps you understand your feelings and see how you respond to impulses. Understanding your beliefs, thoughts, and values will go a long way in helping you be authentic. It will help you keep an open mind to the opinions and backgrounds of others, and you will see how incredible this tool is to bring people closer. Finally, always stay in the present and focus on the tasks at hand. You already have a future plan; now it's time to get with the team and work on things that are in tune with your purpose.

5. Understand Your Personal Values

When you reflect on your life, you allow yourself to become a better leader. You can explain your passions, principles, and values and then can live by them. Knowing your values will give you the drive and passion to inspire others to believe in the same things.

TECHNIQUES TO BUILD AUTHENTICITY

It is clear by now that discovering your authentic style takes hard work. It takes a deep self-reflection to learn the things that are truly important to you. It demands that you dig deep to understand your values so that you can live in them. Mostly, it takes courage to stay true to the person you discover, even when the pressure to conform is high. There are three activities in this section. The first one is meant to help you find your authentic self. The other two are intended to help you figure out whether you are behaving authentically.

It is easy to veer off the path of authenticity, so make a habit of checking yourself to see if you are still on track. The third exercise will help you with that. Since authenticity is so important to confidence, the activities in this chapter are a little longer than those in earlier chapters. They are all hinged on self-reflection. Make sure that you are honest when working on them.

1. Self-reflect Based on the Authenticity Principle

According to the authenticity principle, seven behavioral dimensions reflect how you make decisions. These areas include:

- **How you express your emotions** – The extent to which you restrain yourself or express what you feel.
- **How you use non-verbal communication** – The way you use facial expressions, eye contact, posture, touch, and gestures.
- **The words you use** – Are you formal or informal? What is your vocabulary like? Do you use slang?
- **The way you speak** – Your accent, volume, intonation, pace, and pitch.
- **Your appearance** – How do you present yourself before others? What do you wear? Do you put on accessories? Do you have tattoos? What is your sense of style?
- **The content you share** – What do you reveal

about your thoughts, values, opinions, and ideas?

- **Your actions** – How do you treat people? Who do you speak to, and who do you avoid? How do you self-promote? Who do you defer to?

The goal of this exercise is to use these seven dimensions as a guide to understanding yourself. Find a quiet place and set aside an hour. Bring a pen and notebook or your laptop. Leave behind anything distracting, such as your phone. Reflect on the following questions regarding the seven dimensions and answer them with as much detail as you can. You will answer each of the questions for each dimension.

- *If there were no consequences for how you behave, how would you work out this dimension?*
- *When did you feel inauthentic in this dimension? What was happening? How did you behave and why?*

Once you have answered these questions, reflect on your answers. Which of the seven dimensions is most important to you? What things must you do, and what are you willing to compromise in the different dimensions?

2. Use "Yes" or "No" Questions to Self-appraise

The first exercise gives you a clear path to understanding yourself better. It sets the stage for making more empowered choices, but this exercise gives you greater meaning and clarity. It will help you understand authenticity as the art of telling the truth without spilling your guts. Answer the following questions with a "yes" or "no." Do not overthink your answers.

- *Are you able to share your struggles and fears openly?*
- *Do you own your mistakes without passing blame?*
- *Do you try to prove your perspective as correct?*
- *If someone asks to know your thoughts, do you share everything?*
- *Do you apologize more than once when you make a mistake?*

Reflect on your answers and figure out what they tell you about what you value.

3. Test Your Authenticity on an Ongoing Basis

A major part of authenticity is staying true to your values on an ongoing basis. When you veer off the path, you have to rediscover and reconnect with your authentic self. Through this process, you increase your confidence in yourself and create satisfying relationships. You regain your zest for life and creativity. Use the following questions to help you figure out if you are being your authentic self.

Note that as you continue answering these questions, your authentic self will begin to perk up. Keep exploring and asking the questions of yourself and the world around you. Check-in regularly, and you will start to see the differences between your existing self and your authentic self.

How easy is it for you to make a choice?

When you are truly aligned with who you are, you always know what is best for you. You do not lose sight of the factors that make a decision difficult, but you always know the best path for yourself. When you have difficulties making a choice, it is because the other factors hide the simplicity of your authentic choice. You are not authentic if you make your decisions based on how other people react or if you avoid confrontation.

Do you tell the truth?

Ask yourself how often you bend the truth. How honest are you when describing a situation that has happened? Do your stories shift a bit every time you replay them in your head? Do you allow your emotions to re-interpret events? How do you tell the story to others? Your authentic self does not need to lie. When you bend the

truth, you are walking in insecurity or fear of consequences. If you feel the need to lie, you are not owning
your actions, mistakes, or choices, and you are probably
not happy with them. Your authentic self will not hide
the truth. It allows you to be "you" at all times.

Do your actions align with what you believe?

What do you do every day? At any one moment, ask
yourself whether what you are doing aligns with your
values. If the answer is "yes", you are being authentic. If
it is "no", you are not being true to yourself. Check
regularly to see if your actions and your values match,
then recommit to your values if they do not.

Is your "critical voice" getting louder?

The critical voice gets louder when you are not doing what you know to be right. If it is criticizing you, then you have veered off the path of authenticity. Your authentic voice speaks softly. It is kind, clear, and supportive. Ignore your critical voice for a moment and listen to the voice underneath. Then, follow the advice of your authentic voice.

When asked who you are, do you answer by saying what you do?

Your authentic self is not just the things you have done or do now. It is about who you are without the external trappings. It is your core. If you find yourself having trouble explaining who you are, it is a sign that you have lost touch with your authentic self. Take the time to remind yourself who you are and reconnect with what you love.

If you had a choice, would you still choose to do what you are doing now?

If you are not satisfied with what you do every day, something is wrong. When the things you do don't match with what you want to do, they are not guided by authenticity. When you are authentic, you choose what is best for you. Even when doing something that is not your favorite, you still value it because it is a choice you make from your core. You know you are being authentic when your choices cause you to love what you do and feel satisfied with your life.

Do you feel confused, stressed, anxious, or fearful?

Everyone has low points. You may be stressed after an argument. But if you feel confused, stressed, fearful. or anxious and cannot explain it, you are out of tune. You need to set aside some time for soul searching and uncover what you can do to return to your authentic self.

How frequently do you feel curious?

Curiosity is inevitably tied to authenticity. When you ask questions, you explore the world and experience it deeply. You pay attention to details you might otherwise miss. If you have stopped asking questions, it may be a sign that you have grown content and are veering away from authenticity. Your authentic self wants to be involved and engaged. It wants to determine its truths.

7

GROW YOUR RESILIENCE

Resilience is the power to control your emotions in difficult times. It is the confidence and strength to get through anything that comes your way. If you are resilient, you can overcome any adversity, trauma, or setback and live fully after it has passed. Resilient leaders push themselves and their teams to achieve extraordinary things. Whether it's a project with their clients or in the market, a resilient leader can create drive, pride, and integrity. They keep their energy even under pressure and cope with disruptive change. They know how to bounce back from setbacks without becoming disengaged in their behavior or causing harm to others.

Resilience is about the whole person. You cannot be resilient if your brain and your heart are maligned.

When people close their hearts, they lose empathy, which is necessary for leadership and resilience. Resilience demands that you keep an open heart, be curious about others, and express your feelings. Some people assume that leadership exists in an emotional vacuum. That is not true. The resilient leader has to be fully sold on what they are doing. It is the conviction that they are walking the right path that keeps them going.

Resilience is tied to grit. Resilient people persevere, and they work hard to achieve what they set out to achieve. They are incredibly focused and loyal to what they believe in. Their commitment is long-term. They handle their goals like a marathon rather than a sprint. It also demands that leaders learn to cope with stress. Research shows that stress is not physically harmful. It is the reactions to stress, such as fast breathing and increased heartbeat, which pose a threat. Good leaders know how to manage those. They know how to strike a balance between excess worry and not enough worry, meaning that their approach is always constructive and positive. It energizes them rather than sap their joy. This chapter talks about the importance of being resilient, and what a leader can gain if they are resilient. It then goes into detail about how you can become resilient to be a transformational leader.

The Effects of Resilience

A resilient leader can lessen the burden of stress on themselves and make it easier to achieve their goals. They know how to take challenges in a stride and never lose perspective. Leading a team to success can be very stressful. It is resilience that helps you lift all the pressure off your shoulders. It enables you to figure out how much attention to give to what setback and when to let things be. When you are resilient, you will gain the confidence and strength to overcome whatever stands in the way of your present and your dreams.

Resilience helps you get the talent and skill you need to help you in the different steps toward your goal. A leader needs to let his team know when he needs help, and you cannot do this without resilience. Fortunately, asking for help when you need it has numerous benefits:

- It creates a positive relationship between you and your team.
- It will nurture your employees and create an atmosphere that supports and affirms self-improvement.
- Being resilient will help you to handle the challenges of work relationships.

If you ever find yourself between a rock and a hard place, resilience can help you escape from the situation's stress and think logically.

Imagine a leader who cannot control their emotions. When they are angry, they say whatever comes to mind. Eventually, that would cause them to lose respect in the eyes of their peers. A resilient leader can control their outbursts. They are careful not to create an uncomfortable environment in the workplace with their emotions. Resilience will give you the power of self-control. It will provide you with incredible strength to govern yourself and deal with the problems your team faces. Resilience gives you a voice that cannot be silenced.

Resilient leaders adapt to change.

Resilient leaders can adjust to difficulties quickly. They can clearly see the things that have worked in the past. They know how to apply their experience to the future. They are confident in their ability to evaluate situations to achieve whatever they set their minds to. When you are resilient, you know that sometimes things do not work but that does not mean that they will never work. You never lose faith. You encourage your team to look beyond failure and use it as a stepping-stone to a better future.

Resilient leaders are resourceful.

Resourcefulness helps you improve a situation by coming up with a clever solution to a challenge. A resourceful leader thinks outside the box. Resourcefulness helps you see the big picture and place the small details within it accurately. It does not mean that you can pull off the impossible, but that you can turn unfavorable circumstances in your favor. It allows you to empower others to swim in the murky waters rather than drown. It allows you to accommodate change.

STRATEGIES TO BECOME RESILIENT

Resilience can become second nature but only with enough practice. Think of growing your resilience like a child's first day in kindergarten. The change is big, and most kids are intimidated and scared. Soon enough, though, they make friends and get used to their routine. Growing your resilience will be like that. But it will also demand a commitment to staying resilient. Here are some ways to become resilient:

Develop a Network of Professionals

The idea here is to surround yourself with like-minded people. When the people around you share your values and thoughts, these relationships become a support system. As you work with your team to pursue the same goal, it creates resilience within the team. You all charge one another toward achieving success.

Socialize

Though important, work relationships are not the only relationships you need to grow your resilience. Make a habit of meeting new people. Find common goals and build memories with them. You will be surprised to find that forging new relationships helps build resilience in different areas of your life. The effect will ripple to all other aspects of how you live.

Exercise

Research links exercise to effectiveness in leadership. When you are stressed and pressed for time, that is when you need exercise the most. Staying healthy in stressful times will reduce the strain you feel and increase your ability to deal with stress. Exercise improves your cognitive functions. It is one of the first things you need to work on to become resilient in your life. When you have a regular exercise regime, you reduce the total amount of stress accumulating in your body.

Get Enough Sleep

Many people make the mistake of undervaluing sleep. Caught up in the rush of daily activities, they ignore how much sleep they get until they are burnt out and spiraling out of control. A leader needs to be well-rested and energized as they present themselves to their team. You are a role model, and you need to be in the right state of mind to embody that. Adequate sleep will improve your critical thinking as well as your resilience and problem-solving abilities.

On the other hand, if you are sleep-deprived, you will have a poor memory, slower responses to problems, and a reduced focus on work. It will become harder to make decisions, all of which will affect your resilience.

Find New Perspectives

You are working toward a single goal alongside your team. Focusing on only one perspective could stray you away from your purpose. Make a habit of looking at things differently. Imagine new possibilities, and if you can do that, you will see your problems from different angles. If you shift the lens through which you are looking at a problem, it becomes less daunting.

Live in the Present

It is easy to obsess over what could have been, especially when things do not work out. Do not stress yourself too much over what could have happened. Instead, work with your team on current goals. These are the goals that will compound and help you achieve the kind of future you hope for. You have to deal with them in the present, though. Make a habit of savoring the moments. Research has found that our brains have a negative bias or a natural tendency to mull over the bad things. However, you can train your brain to focus on the positives. Make good memories with your team, and you will see yourself grow in your resilience.

Practice Gratitude

By definition, gratitude is an acknowledgment of value. Try to acknowledge and appreciate your abilities. If you encounter something that you cannot do, it is okay to accept it. You can look at it as valuable information on where your limits are. That way, you have a better outlook on life. When you practice gratitude, it gives you a sense of control over different aspects of life. It helps you focus on the good that you can achieve. It may prompt you to hire people who will complement your skills, which will then help you accomplish whatever you failed to do in the first place.

Find Ways to Relax Your Mind and Body

It may seem counterintuitive, but meditation is actually good for your resilience. It has been proven to calm your senses and increase awareness. Meditate regularly to understand what you are feeling and avoid being controlled by your emotions. Make sure you create some downtime where your focus is yourself. It will help you to develop a resilient personality.

Communicate and Communicate Well

Imagine driving down a freeway, and someone takes a sudden right turn without indicating. That one decision can cause chaos that may take some time to recover from. The same is true for leaders who do not inform others about what they are trying to do. Share your concerns, thoughts, and struggles. Ensure that your team is aware of what you need and ask them to help you achieve it. As a leader, you get to learn from your team in the same way that they learn from you.

TECHNIQUES TO GAIN RESILIENCE

The world is constantly changing. If it's not a new product to embrace, it will be a new technology to master or a new team to manage. You will be required to perform well in a short period. These exercises will equip you to anticipate and handle challenges. They will give you the necessary skills and capabilities to become agile, survive, and thrive despite the obstacles you have to deal with.

Note that it will be easier to handle some challenges more than others; not all challenges are equal. Not all situations will demand that you marshal the same inner resources. While growing your resilience cannot guarantee that you will deal with all challenges well, it guarantees that no change will take you by surprise. It will set you and your team up for success. It will allow you to regulate your responses at all times and to remain resourceful and resilient in the face of a threat.

1. Create a Home Base

A home base is not a physical space. It is a feeling of certainty for yourself. Once you create your home base, it becomes easier to let go of the things you cannot control and choose how to respond to challenges. For example, you can tie your home base to your ability to adapt. That way, as things change, you trust that you will evolve as well. In the face of the challenge, you enter your home base, take stock, and figure out how to develop yourself to match the change. You empower yourself to be resourceful. Here is how to create a home base:

- Slow down and allow yourself time to reflect. Cut the continuous flow of information for a while and do what you have to do to challenge your perception of reality.
- Answer the following questions: What are the facts? What is the trigger? What can you control? What is the worst that could happen? What do you need to be stronger? What are you waiting for?

The very exercise of answering these questions will center you. It will allow you to figure out the way forward and adjust appropriately.

2. Practice Paced Breathing

Sometimes you may have difficulties returning to the baseline — a calm emotional state. When you are experiencing anxiety, paced breathing can help. It sends a message to your brain that you are okay and can deal with whatever is ahead of you. Here is how to go about it:

- Take a minute off your day and focus on your breath.
- Breath in through your nose and exhale from your mouth.
- Take in the air slowly and deeply until your lungs inflate fully.
- Exhale slowly until your lungs are empty.
- Repeat for as long as you need to feel calm.

3. Resist "Thinking Traps"

Sometimes, the thing stopping you from adapting to your challenges is your thinking patterns. Learning how to avoid thinking traps will help you become resilient. Black-and-white thinking is an example of a thinking trap. It has to do with the assumption that things are either perfect or terrible. Other times you could catastrophize and dwell on the worst possible outcome, making it hard for yourself to cope. Whatever thinking trap you are prone to, here is how to resist falling into it:

- **Notice what is happening** – When you start spiraling, catch yourself in the initial steps.

- **Re-center your thoughts** – Ask yourself what the reality is as if you were talking to a friend. Are there gray areas? If so, find them. The idea here is to become as realistic as possible.
- **Use a coping mantra** – Find a simple phrase that you can use to answer your concerns when they surface. For example, you can tell yourself, "I am doing my best, and I will be fine."

8

OVERCOME YOUR LIMITING BELIEFS

Sometimes in life, something happens that is so jarring that you make up a story of why it happened and begin to live by it. This could be anything from the day your boyfriend breaks up with you to when you get fired. You make up a story because it keeps you safe. It allows you to process what has happened without getting walloped by its implications. But we do not make up stories only for bad things. In fact, human beings live within a story. You interpret everything, not just the momentous occasions, within the context of a story. This means that the story you tell yourself could be standing in the way of you becoming a transformational leader.

Let's take Nina's story as an example:

Growing up, Nina was not artistic. Creativity and art are the same in her mind, making her shy of pursuing anything she thinks as creative. A few years ago, she only baked as a hobby. For her, baking was more chemistry than it was creative expression. After a while, she got bored with the redundancy. She started experimenting, learning new skills, and questioning. One day, she asked herself, "If I can do this, what else can I do?". She was lucky enough to begin exploring why she had the limiting belief that she was not artistic. Eventually, within five years, she was able to grow her bakery into a premium experience for her customers.

In this chapter, you will learn what limiting beliefs are, how to find yours, and how to overcome them so that you can grow into the leader you were meant to be. You will find what you need to overturn the narrative in your early life regarding leadership and how to reprogram your thoughts, so they don't hold you back.

WHAT ARE LIMITING BELIEFS?

Have you ever made a statement like "I am not good at writing reports" or "Speaking in public is not my thing"? These are some examples of limiting beliefs. A limiting belief corners you and gives you a false definition — a false sense of self. It is a conviction, state of mind, or belief that you hold as truth, but it limits you in one way or another. It could be about you, how you interact with others, or about the world and how you see things work out.

Generally speaking, a limiting belief can have negative effects on you. It could stop you from making good choices, grabbing new opportunities, or living up to your full potential. In the end, limiting beliefs will keep you in a negative mind frame, stopping you from living the life you desire, or becoming the kind of leader you know you were meant to be. If you think back to your earliest childhood memories, you may recall times when you were fearless. It was those times that curiosity took you to places you otherwise wouldn't go. As you get older, you become familiar with all the rules that you should follow.

You learned the things that are appropriate to say and those that aren't. You learned what you should do and how you are to carry yourself. These rules likely caused you to create limiting beliefs without even being aware of them. The truth is that while you do have to abide by some limitations, you mustn't hold yourself back and clip your wings before you have learned to fly. Knowing your limiting beliefs is about understanding the things inside you that stand in the way of attaining greater heights. It is removing the internal roadblocks so that you are equipped to deal with any external challenges.

Research shows that the first place you draw limiting beliefs from is your family. Growing up, your parents likely had values and morals that they tried to get you to learn. These values came from their familial ideas and beliefs. They might have thought you should follow a given career path or engage with others in a certain way. You end up forming your beliefs based on theirs. For example, if your parents believed that authority should never be challenged, you may have adopted that as a belief. You may believe that you should bear unfair treatment from those in authority or that your employees should never question you.

Secondly, limiting beliefs can also come from how you were educated. Whether you are learning from friends, teachers, or family, they impact what you come to hold as true. They are constantly sharing ideas, beliefs, and information about how they perceive the world. Since you tend to respect these people, you conclude that what they say is true.

Thirdly, you can develop limiting beliefs from your experiences. When you make choices that have consequences, it is common to draw conclusions. For example, if you attempt a specific project and it fails, you might conclude that similar projects will also go wrong.

Negative experiences powerfully shape your limiting beliefs.

STRATEGIES TO OVERCOME YOUR LIMITING BELIEFS

The good thing with limiting beliefs is that they are not written in stone. You have the power to change your beliefs at any time. This is not to say that the process will be easy but committing to the process can make it possible. Here are some ways you can begin overcoming any limiting beliefs:

Put Your Environment in Order

Many people may not know it, but your environment can affect what you believe to be true. For example, when you have a spacious and well-organized environment, you may improve your mood and encourage yourself to think positively. With a tidy environment, you create space to think and acquire clarity. Bringing your environment to order is about removing any clutter that has possibly accumulated over time. You could go as far as redesigning your space so that movement is more efficient. The basic idea is that in ordering your environment, you channel your flow of energy. Keeping a positive energy influences your mindset and helps you focus on positive beliefs and thoughts.

Get Rid of Anything You Do Not Need

The philosophy of minimalism has a lot to lend to a person looking to overcome limiting self-beliefs. Its fundamentals are honesty, clarity, and detachment from material things. Embracing minimalism can help you get rid of false beliefs that keep you from embracing your inner leader. For example, addiction to always adding new clothing to your wardrobe may be tied to a limiting belief about your appearance. You may believe that you are only attractive when you wear the latest fashions. Getting rid of things you do not need will change your mindset and help you become a person who resists peer pressure. It will help reverse your limiting beliefs and live a meaningful lifestyle.

Cultivate Your Curiosity

Limiting beliefs are often tied to closed-mindedness. One way to reverse yours is opening your mind and following your curiosity to where it leads you. It will help you explore the world around you and leave your comfort zone. This ends up expanding your mind and causing you to challenge even more things you have come to hold as true. Curiosity will open room to learn about what others believe and interact with new ideas.

It will allow you to have conversations with people whose backgrounds differ from yours.

Develop Yourself

A transformational leader is constantly growing and inspiring others to become better versions of themselves. If you want better beliefs to guide your choices and thinking, you must keep working on yourself. You have to actively look for growth and development opportunities in different areas of your life. Improving yourself will increase your self-awareness and help you deal with your weaknesses. It will force you to work on your limiting beliefs instead of hoping that they will disappear on their own. Make a habit of reading books whose authors have similar beliefs to those you are trying to develop. Listen to podcasts. Set goals that will help you measure your growth and journal to track your progress.

Affirm Yourself

It can be challenging to stay positive, especially if you are struggling in one area. Positive affirmations help you refocus on what matters. They force you to speak about who you are positively. With time, you start to believe those affirmations. The next chapter will deal with self-talk. However, for positive self-talk, you must remember that limiting beliefs about your identity will stand in the way of you leading from a place of peace. Make sure that your affirmations also celebrate your strengths. That way, you remind yourself how incredible you are and encourage yourself to push further and do more.

TECHNIQUES TO KNOW AND OVERCOME LIMITING BELIEFS

The world is full of beliefs. There are differences among people; this will never change. You have to figure out the beliefs that support the type of leader you want to be. As a rule of thumb, any belief that keeps you from living the life you want is a limiting belief. It does not have to be outrightly negative. It could be a belief about your abilities that you have outgrown. Whatever limiting beliefs you identify through the following exercises need to go. In getting rid of them, you allow yourself to make a life that exceeds your expectations.

Since you are constantly changing, your beliefs also change with you. Some that served you well become less fitting. As such, you need to regularly meditate on yourself and take stock of how you are doing. Finding your limiting beliefs and overcoming them is not a one-time exercise. In other cases, once you change a belief, it may open your eyes to yourself more clearly. You start to see other areas that need improving. Meditating calms you and connects you with your inner self. It gets you past the clutter in your head and allows you to focus on the beliefs you want to embrace. Before you know it, your mind is filled with positivity, and you become a better version of yourself.

The first exercise in the list below will help you identify your limiting beliefs. The other two will help you to begin overcoming those beliefs and start embracing better ones.

1. Identify your Limiting Beliefs Through Reflection

Limiting beliefs are not easy to identify. It may take you a few tries to pin them down accurately. To start, write down your general beliefs. Anything that you feel strongly about should go on the list. Next, prioritize the things that influence your choices every day. Group these beliefs into different categories, such as health, relationships, family, and finances. Once you do this, call them to question. Which beliefs are helping you grow?

You may find it difficult to distinguish between your helpful and limiting beliefs. That's normal. Assess how you behave based on each belief. Identify scenarios where you responded in toxic or damaging ways. Ask yourself why you felt that to be your way forward.

If you look closely enough, you will discover that a limiting belief drives negative responses to an event. For example, if you find that you cannot tell someone that they have offended you, it could be that you believe conflict is bad. That is a limiting belief that may get in the way of having intimate relationships.

As you do this exercise, record any areas where you feel challenged. If you notice that the challenges you have in different areas are recurring, they may point to a major limiting belief. As you go through each point, reflect on what belief you might change and how it would impact your life.

2. Reason with Your Thoughts

As you try to identify your limiting beliefs, you may notice that you have some resistance or fear. If that happens, stop, and reflect. Acknowledge that you are in a low mood for the exercise, then remember that your thoughts are not always the truth. Write down the reasons why you think you have the resistance. What lies are you telling yourself? You will realize that you have tied beliefs to different events in your life. Ask yourself whether they are really true about you.

While reasoning with yourself, look for evidence. Treat your mind like a crime scene. You are a detective who must unravel the truth using clues. The idea here is to know that you have the power to embrace the truth instead of the lies you have told yourself. What evidence do you see that opposes your limiting beliefs? When you see evidence, you can start taking your power back. Rather than blame everyone else for the results you find, you take responsibility.

You alone are in the driver's seat when it comes to your life and thoughts. Feeling stressed and anxious is a result of relinquishing control. Remind yourself that a thought is simply a thought, a feeling is just a feeling. They are not true about you. They pass.

3. Talk to Someone

It might help you to talk through your challenges with someone you trust. If you want to change your limiting story and embrace new, empowering beliefs about the world and yourself, talk with someone who wants the best for you. Talking about these limitations can help you live a life of inspiration and flow. If you don't have such a friend, seek out a counselor or a therapist.

It could be that your limiting beliefs trigger other conditions like depression or anxiety. A professional will help you figure things out. They have the knowledge and resources to help you overcome specific challenges. They can help you trace the limiting beliefs you have adopted across time and equip you with the resources you need to overcome or change them.

9

REFINE YOUR SELF-TALK

S elf-talk is not often discussed among leadership topics, but it is an important skill to master. Leaders are not immune to negative self-talk. While you might imagine that stepping into a leadership role imbues you with a positive self-track record, it is not uncommon for many people to struggle. In fact, negative self-talk could be precisely the thing stopping you from reaching your leadership potential. Pressures in your world and a strong sense of responsibility for others can create a lot of negative chatter. How many times have you said a variation of the below statements?

- *I am as lost as others, but I cannot show that.*
- *I was unable to sleep. I was worried.*

- *I have no idea why I was picked for this job. I am not up to it.*
- *I don't know what to do next, and I am afraid I will make the wrong choice.*

This chapter recognizes that leaders are humans too. They all struggle with similar worries and doubts. Yet, influential leaders have learned to funnel their fears and doubts into something constructive. They have tools and techniques they use to deal with their internal dialogue. They recognize that self-doubt, fear, and catastrophizing can be enemies in their leadership journey. They know how to deal with their negative emotions, so they aren't ruled by them. They can shift their thinking toward the positive.

This chapter is about that. It is meant to help you banish your inner critic and learn how to be positive and productive. It will help you to be willing to put in the time and effort necessary to improve yourself. You will learn how to reprogram your self-talk for the sake of your leadership success.

WHAT IS SELF-TALK?

Self-talk is your inner dialogue. It is influenced by your subconscious and reveals your questions, beliefs, thoughts, and ideas. It is something that you naturally do as long as you are awake. Becoming aware of your self-talk and making it positive is a way to increase your self-confidence and deal with negative emotions. People who master positive self-talk become more productive, motivated, and confident.

Self-talk is either positive or negative. It can be distressing or encouraging. Much of how you talk to yourself depends on your personality. Optimists tend to be more positive and hopeful while pessimists tend to be more negative. Still, regardless of your natural tendencies, you can take advantage of the power of positive self-talk. You can learn to shift your inner dialogue and become more positive. Research shows that optimistic people tend to have a better quality of life. In refining your self-talk, you improve your life.

Researchers also found that self-talk is not about the things you say to yourself. It also includes the language you use when speaking to yourself. Language plays a huge role in self-talk. One researcher recommends that you refer to yourself in the third person or by name when speaking to yourself. For most people, the default is to talk to yourself using the first-person "I" or "me". Other researchers suggest personifying the negative voices in your head. In giving them a name, you step away from them and take away some of their power. Separating yourself from self-talk allows you to think about it objectively. That way, you can process the event in question without getting stressed and anxious.

Self-talk enhances your general well-being and performance. Based on research, athletes who have positive self-talk perform better. They can endure and do more than they think possible. Powerful self-talk also improves your vitality and satisfaction with life. Optimistic people are less prone to stress and distress. They are able to talk themselves down when their emotions ride high. They can calm down and figure out a solution that makes things better.

Positive self-talk even influences your physical well-being. It improves your immune function, reduces pain, improves your cardiovascular health, and lowers the risk of death, according to research conducted on athletes. It is unclear why optimistic athletes do better than their pessimistic counterparts, but research shows they have mental skills that make problem-solving easier. Optimists think differently and are able to cope with challenges.

Negative self-talk can be divided into different categories, including:

- **Magnifying** – When you magnify, your focus is on the negative aspects of a given situation, so much so that you do not see the positives.

- **Personalizing** – A person who is prone to personalizing takes all the blame for things that go wrong.
- **Polarizing** – When you polarize, you see the world and events as either good or bad. There is no middle ground.
- **Catastrophizing** – A person who is catastrophizing expects only the worst from events. They do not rely on reason or logic.

Turning your negative self-talk into positive self-talk takes practice. Recognizing it is the first step. Here are some examples of negative self-talk:

- *I will disappoint everyone else if I change my mind.*
- *I have embarrassed myself with this failure.*
- *When I didn't cover that in the report, I let everyone on my team down.*
- *There is no way this will work.*
- *I am new at this, so I will mess it up.*

HOW EFFECTIVE LEADERS HARNESS THE POWER OF SELF-TALK

Positive self-talk takes practice. It is not an instinct for most people. Yet, effective leaders have learned to shift their inner dialogue to make it uplifting and encouraging. They embody the following qualities:

They can identify the traps for negative self-talk.

Different scenarios trigger different things. Some of them increase your self-doubt and make you more prone to talk to yourself negatively. Effective leaders have learned how to identify these traps. They know how to prepare for work events that tend to be difficult for them. They can pinpoint when they experience the most negative self-talk, and they can prepare for it.

They check in with their feelings.

During difficult events, it is easy to get carried away. People who have mastered their self-talk check in with themselves. They take the time to evaluate their self-talk and determine how to turn it around if it takes a negative turn.

They can find humor.

Sometimes, all you need to do to shift your perspective is to find the humor. Effective leaders know that laughter can relieve tension and stress. When they realize that they need a positive self-talk boost, they find ways to laugh. They have go-to material that helps to cheer them up. This could be anything from listening to a comedian to watching funny animal videos.

They surround themselves with positive people.

Whether you are aware of it, the people you hang around with impact how you view yourself and the world. You can absorb their emotions and outlook. Confident wizards surround themselves with positive people whenever possible.

They affirm themselves.

Sometimes, an inspiring image or a moving quote may be all you need to redirect your energy and thoughts. Effective leaders know this. They invest the necessary effort to make it easier to affirm themselves. This can be anything from posting small reminders in their office to adjusting the wallpaper on their smartphone.

They do not think only of themselves.

Leaders who have mastered their self-talk are not all about "me", "myself" and "I". Even in their thinking, they refer to themselves in the second person. As such, they see tasks as challenges rather than threats. They make better first impressions because they are not always wrapped up in themselves when interacting with others.

They talk to themselves as they would with a close friend.

Confident wizards have learned how to treat themselves as someone they care for and that they are responsible for helping. They do not yell at themselves. Even when they make a mistake, they do not swear at themselves. Effective leadership is about embracing constructive self-talk. Such leaders realize that dysfunctional self-talk squelches their creativity, so instead, they offer themselves motivation and reassurance.

They watch for distorted patterns of thought.

Effective leaders do not assume that their feelings and thoughts are objective and aligned with reality. They watch out for black-and-white thinking, overgeneralizing, and catastrophizing. They know that their cognitive distortions may have been a mechanism to survive, but they have long outgrown the stress they tried to survive. They are careful not to let those distortions affect their life and decision-making.

ACTIVITIES TO REFINE YOUR SELF-TALK

The good news about negative self-talk is that it does not need to be your reality forever. You can learn to recognize your thoughts for what they are and avoid letting them lead you astray. Positive self-talk is both a product of and a factor in self-confidence. How you talk to yourself depends on how you feel about your-self, and it can affect your feelings about yourself. The following activities are meant to help you identify your negative self-talk and turn it into positive self-talk. Think of them as a way to secure your mask before you help others.

When the world and your team are in crisis mode, it may feel selfish to focus on your self-talk. Self-talk easily seems inconsequential. However, mastering your self-talk is a form of crisis training. For a transforma-tional leader, mastering self-talk is about knowing the exits, staying calm, securing their mask, and then helping others. It is about learning how to help yourself so that you are in a good place to help others. It is one way to help you show up as your best self before your team and manage everything around you confidently.

You can do some of the following activities before a crisis while others are useful in the eye of the storm. Refining your self-talk will take time and practice, but you will soon reap the benefits if you keep at it.

It is also worth noting that refining your self-talk is like any other habit you try to learn. It requires repetition. Substituting your negative self-talk with more accurate and hopeful self-talk demands a commitment to consciously repeating the following exercises even when you do not feel like it. This is simply the process of creating new thought patterns.

1. Identify Your Negative Self-talk

A critical step to refining your self-talk is to recognize your type of negative thinking. That way, you know what to work on to make a positive change. Think back to the different types of self-talk. Which one are you most prone to? Can you pick up specific examples? During this step, you will use your journal entry to clarify your beliefs. Self-talk can be tied to your limiting beliefs. If you are having trouble seeing specific examples, observe how you respond to yourself in a situation where a limiting belief is at play. Remind yourself that everything you need on your leadership journey is on the other side of your limiting beliefs and negative self-talk.

Another way you can identify your negative self-talk is to use your inventory of values. Often, you will berate yourself when you go against something you value. If you value family but spend all your day at work, you will likely criticize yourself for that choice. Whatever is on your list of values, find the associated negative self-talk, and write it down. While you're at it, look at your goals. Which goals have you not met? What do you say to yourself about not achieving them yet?

2. Reframe Your Negative Thoughts

In reframing, you take a negative thought and make it positive. It is about converting your self-talk from negative to positive. At the beginning of the chapter, we listed some examples of negative self-talk. Here is how they sound when they are reframed:

> **Negative:** I will disappoint everyone else if I change my mind.
> *Reframe: I have the power to change my mind. Others will get it.*

> **Negative:** I have embarrassed myself with this failure.
> *Reframe: I am proud that I tried. It took courage.*

> **Negative:** When I didn't cover that on the report, I let everyone on my team down.
> *Reframe: Our work is a team job. We lose and win together.*

> **Negative:** There is no way this will work.
> *Reframe: I can give this everything I have and make it work.*

> **Negative:** I am new at this, so I will mess it up.

Reframe: This is a great opportunity for me to learn and grow.

Negative: I envy my friend's success; she got promoted fast.
Reframe: I am happy for my friend, and I will not compare my situation with her.
After finding out your negative self-talk, reframe each of them, and choose to focus on enabling beliefs.

3. Keep a Self-talk Track

Record the times you fall into negative self-talk. How much did it take you to switch gears? How do you feel about it? Keep a journal log for a few days. It will help you to track your progress. After a while, find out which of your thoughts are the majority in one day — the negative or the positive?

4. Do an Active Reset

An active reset can help you to derail your negative self-talk in the heat of the moment. It is an exercise to help you stop the negative thoughts before they balloon and cause your mood to plummet. Here is how you do the reset:

- Stop and recognize the negative thoughts once they begin.
- Question yourself. Figure out why you are thinking as you are. Is there evidence?
- Use a reframe. Use your list of reframed self-talk to see the situation from a different perspective.
- Act. Decide on an empowering way forward.

10

LOVE AND CARE FOR YOURSELF

A few decades ago, talking about love within leadership theories was unheard of. Today, with Gen Z and millennial workers wanting more meaning and purpose out of work, the concept has found its way. Yet, the only reason you should take self-love seriously in the workplace is not external. In fact, external benefits like increased employee engagement are the icing on the cake. The cake is who you become as a result. If you are like most people, you are very critical of yourself. You do not believe that you are allowed to make mistakes. You set unreasonable expectations and hold yourself and others to them. In doing that, you induce resentment and stress on yourself and those you lead.

This chapter acknowledges leaders as imperfect beings. It is about allowing yourself space to struggle, grow, learn, and become self-fulfilled in the context of effective leadership. It is about ultimately growing your confidence by learning empathy and compassion. Many people find it easy to be compassionate and empathetic when dealing with others but struggle with treating themselves the same way. Yet, empathy and compassion toward yourself are at the heart of self-love, and self-love is a key to living and leading well.

This chapter looks beyond basic styles of leadership and equips you with an evolutionary vehicle for transformational leadership. It deals with a topic that is often ignored when it comes to leadership training sessions and talks — self-love. You will learn what it is, and why it is a prerequisite for great leadership. You will find techniques and strategies to help you learn and care for yourself throughout your leadership journey.

WHAT IS SELF-LOVE?

The leader who has learned to love and care for themselves becomes fully engaged with their purpose and surroundings. Love motivates. It inspires. It creates and gives purpose. As such, it plays an integral role in leadership. Such a leader electrifies everyone around them.

They radiate an energy that inspires others. When you walk into a meeting confident in your skin, this equates to a strong presence. People notice, and they feel better around you.

Self-love is not like romantic love, but it is about channeling energy toward your goals and yourself. Love loses its external focus and originates from within, making it more malleable and active. It becomes a way to interact with the world and channel energy on an object without depending on it. Self-love is a conscious and active mode of being and defines how you see everything and carry yourself.

Since the interaction between self-love and leadership is a fairly new concept, it pays to talk about what self-love is not. Self-love is not arrogance or narcissism. Self-love enables you to love others. It does not hinder your ability to care for them. The narcissist lacks healthy self-esteem and is selfish to feed their desire for attention and praise; the self-loving leader has high self-esteem. They are confident in their interactions because they know their worth and can maintain their happiness. Because they are not reliant on others' praise, they can celebrate their growth and success, understanding that value is not directly linked with competence.

Even though the ties between leadership and self-love are still being explored, it is clear that qualities like authenticity and the ability to inspire, which are primary to leadership, also require self-love. Self-love ties together different traits of leadership and unites different styles despite the tension between them. It can pull teams together through reliability, empathy, and self-sacrifice. Self-love often gets a bad reputation from those who see it as selfish. The truth is that it is the foundation for giving generously and mature living.

Self-love is about giving importance to your well-being. It demands that you care for your mental, emotional, and physical health. You are always answering the question, "What do I need to operate at my best?". Self-love is about trusting yourself, drawing boundaries, and having a deeper connection with your inner being, thus fostering your connection with others. When a self-loving individual walks into a room, they are comfortable in their skin. They have a strong presence that causes others to feel free and comfortable.

Without self-love, you are constantly mulling over what you lack. You look for affirmation and validation from others to fulfill the part of you that feels unworthy. At its worst, a lack of self-love can turn you into a bully, picking on others so that you feel better about yourself. If you are a leader whose internal person is constantly plagued with negative thoughts, it will translate into your company culture. Imagine your inner person as a cup. If you love yourself, this cup is full because you recognize that your natural state is love, and you work to maintain it. Without self-love, you believe your cup is empty, so you constantly wish others would fill it.

At work, this can look like taking feedback personally, being always in need of validation for the work you need, or relying on your income or status to feel important. The list is long. When you do not love yourself, you rely on external factors to make you feel good. This means that you do not really enjoy relationships, status, or success. Conversely, when your needs are met, you trust yourself and others. The culture in your team can be based on trust. Self-love is at the heart of authenticity, empathy, and the ability to listen.

The idea of self-love is the question of focus. What if rather than fixating on what you do not like about yourself, you obsessed over the things you love? Many people find it easy to care for others, but they do not offer the same amount of love to themselves. As a leader, the most courageous act of goodwill you can offer others starts with the amount of love you can offer yourself. To step forward, you must love yourself enough to believe that you bring something of value to your team, company, and even the world. It is impossible to make an impact without this belief.

Self-love is about strengthening the tender places in you with self-confidence while you pursue growth. It is loving the person you are as you seek your highest self. Many people hope to love others without loving themselves. They gloss over the aspects of who they are that are annoying, imperfect, quirky, or unseemly. They hope that loving everyone would smooth the rough edges. Yet, living like that is dangerous. When you do not love yourself, other people's appraisals and ideas matter to you more than your own. You blindly follow other people's guidance. They determine whether you are worthy and loveable.

Missing self-love means missing opportunities. Without self-love, you do not recognize good things coming your way. Opportunities seem too good for you, so you let them slide. When you love yourself, you believe that you are worth more than what people are willing to give. You never ignore your desire to be accepted by others. You understand that the most important story of love is the one you write with yourself.

HOW TO LOVE AND CARE FOR YOURSELF

Loving yourself is both redemptive and powerful. It is through self-love that you value your strengths, gifts, knowledge, and capabilities, trusting that they are unique. Martin Luther King Jr. once said that we must discover where the power of love lies — in redemption. And when we discover the redemptive power of love, we make the world new. By loving yourself, you make your life better. You glow from within, and that fire highlights your best qualities and attracts the best from others. How then do you begin to do that?

Do Not Self-sabotage

Self-sabotage is about undermining your own values and goals. It is knowing that something is genuinely good for you, but then doing something that goes against it. Effective leaders do not consciously self-sabotage. They do what they know they need to do to be where they want to be.

Teach Others Love by Setting Boundaries

Boundaries are important. They teach other people what you are okay with and what you will not abide by. Effective leaders know where they end, and others begin. They are not afraid to set boundaries and take action when boundaries are constantly crossed. They know that those boundaries are actually a way to love others.

Stop Comparing Yourself with Others

Many people are socialized to be competitive, so comparing themselves with others flows naturally. Yet, that can stand in the way of self-love. There is no point in comparing yourself because there is no one else like you. Instead, focus on who you are and who you want to become. That energy shift will help you feel free.

Do Not Worry About the Opinions of Others

The same reason you shouldn't compare yourself with others is also why you shouldn't worry so much about society's expectations of you. Make peace with the fact that you cannot make everyone happy. The time you spend trying is only wasting a resource you could otherwise dedicate to becoming your highest self. Part of this will mean that you let yourself make mistakes. Many people believe that nobody is perfect but treat themselves as though they were. As you take on more responsibilities, you will feel more pressure to never fail. Yet, it is important to ease the pressure on yourself. Instead, remind yourself that mistakes are a place for growth. Embrace the fact that you are constantly changing and that who you are today will be different tomorrow.

Divorce Your Value From Your Looks

So many things in the world are designed to distract you from this attempt – advertisements for products online, the pictures you see of the people meant to be of value and so forth. All seem to be wholly centered on looks. Yet, if you are to transcend the ordinary, you must deal with your internalized sexism. You are valuable because you are the person you are, not because of how you look. If you understand this truth, you will dress in a way that makes you feel good, confident, happy, and comfortable.

Say Goodbye to the Toxic

Not everyone has learned to take responsibility for the things they put out into the world. If you notice someone around you bringing toxicity and refusing to take responsibility, loving yourself will require that you take a step back from them. Do not be afraid to do it. It may be painful, but it is important to protect your energy.

Process Your Fears

Making mistakes is natural, and so is feeling afraid. Do not reject your fears. Instead, work to understand them. Evaluating and interrogating your fears will give you clarity. It will reveal the issues in your life that cause anxiety, which will help to alleviate it. As you process your fears, you will learn to trust your decision-making abilities. Often, fearful people doubt their ability to do what is right. As you face your fears, you will know what is best. You will embolden yourself to advocate for what your heart wants.

Take the Opportunities That Come Your Way

The timing will never be perfect to begin that project you wanted to start. Realize the setup may never be ideal. That should not hold you back from achieving your dreams. Rather, it should empower you to seize the moment.

Put Yourself First

One way to grow in self-love is to be bold enough to put yourself first. Women, especially, get accustomed to putting others first. While there is a place and time for self-sacrifice, you should not make it a habit. It will cost you your emotional and mental well-being. Spare time to decompress and recharge, whether that means spending your day in bed or being outdoors.

ACTIVITIES TO DEVELOP SELF-LOVE

Looking at how you relate with yourself can be scary if you are doing it for the first time. This is why a lot of people avoid it. Most people go as far as dismissing the idea and faking an issue with the concept of self-love. Others assume that they love themselves by default. The exercises in this section make no such assumptions. They challenge you to know your inner being and how you relate with yourself. The path to self-love involves a willingness to be honest with yourself and to see things clearly. It takes a lot of courage to confront the parts of you that you need to heal.

1. List All the Things You Love

This activity is simple. Carve out about 10 minutes. Find a quiet place to sit with a piece of paper and pen in hand. Make a list of everything you love. Do not leave anything out. How long did it take you to list yourself? What does that tell you about how much you love yourself?

2. Self-love Question Journaling

Research has found that there are some questions you can ask yourself to grow your self-love and begin to feel confident. In a journal, answer the below questions.

The more time you take to think about them and yourself (as they direct), the better you will feel.

- *If you stuck to your goal for the next three months, how would your life be different?*
- *What is one tiny thing you can do today to help give you more control of your life?*
- *What can you start doing to feel closer to your loved ones?*

3. Exercise

Physical exercise can go a long way toward helping you love yourself. Pushing yourself to exercise increases your mood, mental strength, and self-love. Pick one physical activity that you love to do. How will it help you feel better about yourself and your body? Commit to doing it every day for the next 30 days. It could be something as simple as jumping rope or taking a 30-minute walk every day.

4. Celebrate Your Successes

Make a list of things you have accomplished that you feel proud of. This exercise will remind you how amazing you are. If you already achieved something difficult once, you can do it again.

11

THE TAKEAWAYS

Now that you have read this book, you understand what it really means to be a confident leader. You have everything you need to win the internal battles and truly lead from within. You know that a leader doesn't delegate but instead encourages, inspires, and teaches. You understand why you have a team. Your team exists to work with you, not for you. You are just as much a part of the team as the next member. Still, you appreciate that a team looks to you for guidance because they want to become better in their talents and skills.

You know the value of authenticity in building proper relationships. People need to know that they can trust you even as they follow your lead. You have a thorough understanding of why resilience is important. It helps you solve all the problems that come your way. You are now well placed to revolutionize leadership. You have the tools to seek out, create, and support transformational change in your leadership. You can do things differently. You can lead yourself and lead from a place of authenticity, inspiring others to show up authentically. You can step out and be more than a typical manager.

The call now is to bring those skills to others. It is to lead in a way that meets people where they are and elevates them to a higher ideal of themselves. It is your turn to lead in a way that positively impacts others. The magic is that in leading this way, it forces you to keep learning. You have to upgrade your approaches and views. This will be a constant thing in your leadership. You will grow and evolve and then you will grow some more.

This book had no prescriptions. By now, you can see that growing in your leadership is a process. It calls you to participate and give yourself wholly to it. Hopefully, now, you can ask yourself these questions:

- *How am I changing myself? How am I impacting others?*

- *What personal beliefs about leadership do I have to challenge to serve others?*
- *How am I making it easy for other people to transform?*

By now, you understand your competencies. You know what areas you can focus on to grow. You realize that your work is not a set of skill sets isolated from other people. You see the impact of your choices and understand how much more it matters that you are true to the spirit of leadership. Now that you are self-aware, you understand why this quality is valuable. You know why you need to share a purpose with your team to create a loving, nurturing, and thriving environment. What then?

The onus is on you to apply these techniques to your work environment. It is now your turn to step into your role as the leader your team needs to achieve your dreams and focus on your purpose in life. You will be surprised by the response. When you are thinking about applying these techniques, ask yourself every day how you show up for your team. Consider the following three areas of impact:

1. Action

How are you showing up to your team in terms of how you see the members, approach conflict, and contribute to work? Are you able to shift from the role of an individual contributor to a leader? Are you creating opportunities for development inside the team? Do you build on the feedback you receive?

2. Influence

Do you understand the force you bring to your team? Are you able to recognize the fact that your approach can incite action in your team?

3. Energy

Do you know that you largely set the tone for your team? Are you aware that you drive your team's mindset? When you feel lost and disconnected from your authentic self, other people in your team will too.

Within these areas, think about how you present yourself and your contribution to the collective mindset. Consider how to maintain momentum. Do not forget that developing all the aspects of a confident wizard takes time and continuous practice. Dedicate yourself to creating a meaningful experience for everyone you touch.

THE EXERCISES

At the end of each chapter in this book, you have encountered different activities. There are a total of 35 exercises. If possible, do all of them. If you are pressed for time, focus on finding your authentic self, finding your purpose, and then doing at least one of the activities in the other chapters. As a final activity, look at the journal you have been using throughout this book. What have you learned about yourself? Which areas do you want to work on? How can you get started?

You have everything you need to become a confident wizard. You can unlock the magic in you. Go forth and change the world!

CONCLUSION

Confidence, or a lack of it, is something that comes up over and over in life. When you enter a job interview, you are not likely to be hired if you do not self-promote to some extent. Without confidence in who you are, how will your potential employer know you are right for the job? This is true throughout your career. When you get your first promotion, your job description changes. You have to learn new skills and hone some of those you already had. Doing this requires confidence.

When you have a new team to manage, you need more confidence than you needed when you were simply a member of a team. People with confidence often succeed, while those without it do not put themselves out there. Confident people have a sense of how important they are in the lives of others. They know that they leave something of themselves with everyone they interact with, so they step out, determined to leave a positive impact.

This is the essence of the confident wizard. In this book, you have explored what exactly makes a true leader. You know the differences between a leader by title and a genuine leader. You also understand the things that contribute to self-confidence:

- Self-awareness
- Self-esteem
- Sense of Purpose
- Authenticity
- Resilience
- Self-talk
- Personal Beliefs
- Self-love

The format of this book is such that each of the aspects received a chapter of its own. From reading and working on the different aspects, you are now self-aware, have high self-esteem, and know what it is like to live with purpose. You step out, ready to live an authentic life, and it does not faze you when you face failure or challenges because you are resilient. You know that you have what it takes to overcome and adapt. For you, failure is not final. You have identified your limiting beliefs and know how to overcome them. You talk to yourself like you are someone you care about, and you know how to love and care for yourself.

As a confident wizard, you know what it takes to face the battles within and emerge victorious. You have everything you need to groom others to become better versions of themselves. What are you going to do with this information? Will you rise to the occasion and change the world?

You can begin your journey by leaving a review of this book on Amazon to let others know how it changed your life.

PRAISE FOR MARLENE GONZALEZ

Dear Reader,

I hope you like it!

As a self-publishing author, I rely on readers like you to help promote my work and serve humanity better by doing my best to write, share, coach and train the next generation of leaders like you.

Please, consider posting an online review on Amazon, a short review, audio, or a picture highlighting the page you enjoyed the most. Book reviews are essential to any book. They help potential buyers make confident decisions when getting and buying books.

Unlock the leader in you.

Your coach, Marlene Gonzalez.

ABOUT THE AUTHOR

Marlene Gonzalez is the founder and the president of Life coaching group LLC. focusing on Leadership development and executive coaching. She passionately pursues one vision- "To advance, develop and promote minority leaders." She is a renowned executive coach and facilitator. She is the author of the coaching series Leadership Wizard; "Number 1 New Release book in the Education and Leadership category". Her book series specializes in transformational leadership topics such as:

- *Leadership Wizard. The Nine Dimensions. Unlock the Leader in You. The Discipline of Coaching Yourself to Fearlessly Lead, Influence, Inspire and Empower Others.*

- *Assertive Wizard. How To Boost Confidence, Get Your Message Across, And Speak With Impact.*
- *Change Wizard. Master The Art Of Leading Change And Working Together for a Common Purpose.*
- *Confident Wizard.* Turn Self Doubt Into Confidence: The Ultimate Guide To Lead With Authenticity, Purpose, and Resilience.

Once you master these and many other topics she covers, you can transform your life and become a more successful leader. In addition, you will find that her books have a straight-to-the-point approach and easy to implement actions. She is passionate about sharing her insights and resources on transformational leadership through a combination of Insights Discovery, the psychology of C. G. Jung, her corporate career experience and her professional coaching expertise.

González held many executive corporate positions in the US, Europe, and Latin America. She is the former Senior Director of Global Training, Learning, and Development for McDonald's Corporation. Marlene holds a BS, an Executive MBA/PAG, and a graduate diploma on managerial Issues in the global enterprise from Thunderbird University. www. marlenegonzalez.com

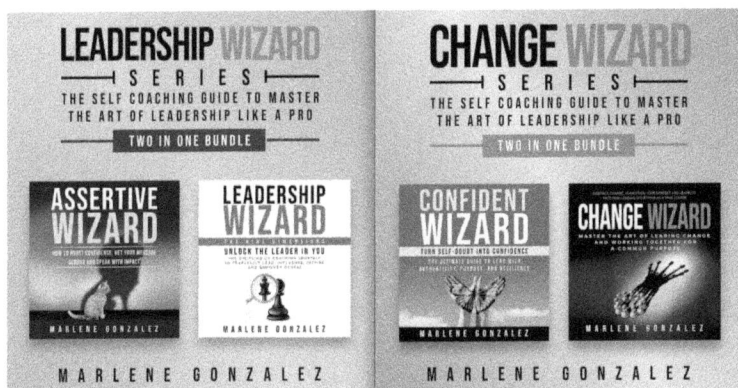

REFERENCES

10 tips for improving your self-esteem. (n.d.). Welcome to ReachOut.com | ReachOut Australia. Retrieved from https://au.reachout.com/articles/10-tips-for-improving-your-self-esteem

17 self-awareness activities and exercises (+ test). (2019, December 18). PositivePsychology.com. Retrieved from https://positivepsychology.com/self-awareness-exercises-activities-test/#questions

25 boosting self esteem questions. (2020, May 20). Online Coaching. Retrieved from https://www.coaching-online.org/self-esteem-questions/

A 4-Ingredient recipe for leadership success in 2021. (2021, April 21). Training Industry. Retrived from https://

trainingindustry.com/articles/leadership/a-4-ingredient-recipe-for-leadership-success-in-2021/

5 exercises for building emotional resilience. (2021, March 23). National Gaucher Foundation. Retrieved from https://www.gaucherdisease.org/blog/5-exercises-for-building-emotional-resilience/

6 important questions to assess your level of grit and resiliency. (2016, August 19). You Have A Calling. Restrieved from https://youhaveacalling.com/emotional-health/6-important-questions-know-resilient

6 ways to start boosting your self-confidence today. (n.d.). Verywell Mind. Retrieved from https://www.verywellmind.com/how-to-boost-your-self-confidence-4163098

7 steps to boost your self-esteem. (2020, July 14). Mayo Clinic. Retrieved from https://www.mayoclinic.org/healthy-lifestyle/adult-health/in-depth/self-esteem/art-20045374

7 strategies to boost your leadership skills through self-awareness. (2021, May 14). Insperity. Retrieved from https://www.insperity.com/blog/self-awareness/

7 ways to find more meaning and purpose in your life. (n.d.). Verywell Mind. Retrieved from https://www.

verywellmind.com/tips-for-finding-your-purpose-in-life-4164689

8 steps to become more resilient | Center for creative leadership. (2021, April 23). CCL. Retrieved from https://www.ccl.org/articles/leading-effectively-articles/8-steps-help-become-resilient/

Are you being your authentic self? 8 questions to ask yourself to find out! (2020, December 30). Stand InBalance. Retrieved from https://standinbalance.com/authentic-self/

Ask yourself 5 questions to ensure you're being authentic. (2016, May 11). Inc.com. Retrieved from https://www.inc.com/sylvia-lafair/ask-yourself-5-questions-to-ensure-you-re-being-authentic.html

Authentic leadership – To thine own self be true. (n.d.). Global leader in learning and development solutions — Insights. Retrieved from https://www.insights.com/us/resources/authentic-leadership/?keywords=&resourceType=7622bd07-7d65-43b0-a9c4-468340318516&subjectMatter=&page=+1&sortType=newest¤tUmbracoPageId=3986

Braden Michelle. (2018). Forbes. Retrieved from https://www.forbes.com/sites/forbescoachescouncil/2018/03/13/seven-ways-to-develop-your-authentic-leadership-style/?sh=7bc1bc1669e6

Cashman, K. (2017, November 9). *8 principles of purpose-driven leadership.* SUCCESS. Retrieved from https://www.success.com/8-principles-of-purpose-driven-leadership/

Congruence is what separates the most influential leaders from everyone else. Here's why. (2018, June 20). Inc.com. Retrieved from https://www.inc.com/matthew-jones/congruence-is-what-separates-most-influential-leaders-from-everyone-else-heres-why.html

Folkman Joseph. (2017). Forbes. Retrieved from https://www.forbes.com/sites/joefolkman/2017/04/06/new-research-7-ways-to-become-a-more-resilient-leader/?sh=2cd851b57a0c

Hawthorne effect — SAGE research methods. (2010). SAGE Research Methods: Find resources to answer your research methods and statistics questions. Retrieved from https://methods.sagepub.com/reference/encyc-of-research-design/n174.xml#:~:text=The%20term%20Hawthorne%20effect%20refers,draw%20regarding%20relationships%20between%20variables

How to find your life purpose in 4 easy steps. (2021, January 5). Jessica DW | Find Your Purpose. Retrieved from https://jessicadw.com/blog/find-your-purpose

Johnson, A. (2015, February 25). *7 powerful questions to help you find your life purpose.* Lifehack. Retrieved from https://www.lifehack.org/articles/communication/7-questions-help-you-find-your-life-purpose.html

Jungian psychology: The eight attitudinal functions. (2020, October 26). DISCOVER YOURSELF. Retrieved from https://discoveryourself.com/jungian-psychology-the-eight-function-attitudes/

Kruse Kevin. (2013). Forbes. Retrieved from https://www.forbes.com/sites/kevinkruse/2013/05/12/what-is-authentic-leadership/?sh=17b89085def7

Kulzow David. (2014). *LEADING FROM WITHIN: Building Organizational Leadership Capacity.* International Economic Development Council— International Economic Development Council. Retrieved from https://www.iedconline.org/clientuploads/Downloads/edrp/Leading_from_Within.pdf

The most potent Gen-Z entrepreneurial panel assembled. (2018, August 25). Inc.com. Retrieved from https://www.inc.com/benjamin-p-hardy/the-most-potent-gen-z-entrepreneurial-panel-assembled.html

Navigating the pressures of working life through resilient leadership. (2015, February 27). IMD business school. Retrieved from https://www.imd.org/research-knowledge/articles/resilient-leadership-navigating-the-pressures-of-modern-working-life/

Resilient leadership: Cultivating greatness at work. (2020, April 1). Insperity. Retrieved from https://www. insperity.com/blog/resilient-leadership/

Search, C. E. (2021, May 10). *The 10 characteristics of a purpose driven leader.* Collingwood Executive Search. Retrieved from https://www.collingwoodsearch.co.uk/ our-insights/board-insights/the-10-characteristics-of- a-purpose-driven-leader/#:~:text=Purpose% 2Ddriven%20leadership%20is%20defined,purposeful% 20performance%20%2D%20make%20it%20happen

Self-aware leader. (n.d.). Global leader in learning and development solutions. Insights. Retrieved from https://www.insights.com/us/products/self-aware- leader/

Thakrar Monica. (2019). Forbes. Retrieved from https://www.forbes.com/sites/forbescoachescouncil/ 2019/09/10/what-does-it-take-to-become-an- authentic-leader/?sh=1dc1afd96e26

Thomson Henry. (2006). High Performing Systems, Inc.: Providing consulting, training and assessments to help organizations, teams and leaders excel. Retrieved from https://www. hpsys.com/Personality_JungsFunction.html

Top 11 benefits of self-awareness according to science. (2019, September 4). PositivePsychology.com. Retrieved from https://positivepsychology.com/benefits-of-self-awareness/

Uncover your authentic self with this simple exercise. (2020, June 30). Ritu Bhasin | Award-Winning Life Coach, Speaker & Author. Retrieved from https://ritubhasin.com/blog/uncover-your-authentic-self

What is self-leadership? Models, theory and examples. (2020, November 20). PositivePsychology.com. Retrieved from https://positivepsychology.com/self-leadership/

www.ingramcontent.com/pod-product-compliance
Lightning Source LLC
Chambersburg PA
CBHW020810300326
41914CB00077B/1791/J